Paying
Attention
to
God

Discernment
in Prayer

Paying
Attention
to
God

William A. Barry, SJ

AVE MARIA PRESS
Notre Dame, Indiana 46556

First printing, January, 1990
Fifth printing, January, 1999
53,000 copies in print

Imprimi Potest
Very Rev. Robert E. Manning, S.J., Provincial
Society of Jesus of New England

Chapters 1, 3, 7, 8, 12, 13 and 15 are adapted from articles first published in *The Tablet*; chapters 9 and 11 from articles first published in *The Church World*, Maine's Catholic weekly; chapters 10 and 14 from articles first published in *America*; chapters 4, 5 and 6 from articles first published in *Review For Religious*; chapter 2 from an article first published in *Sisters' Today*. All are used here with permission of the editors.

International Standard Book Number: 0-87793-414-2
0-87793-413-4 (pbk.)

Library of Congress Catalog Card Number: 89-85963

Book Design: Elizabeth J. French

Printed and bound in the United States of America

To all those men and women
who have trusted me with that most precious gift
their experience of the Mystery we call God
I dedicate this book
with affection and gratitude

Contents

Foreword

I am convinced that the Mystery we call God wants a personal relationship with every person. In this world we encounter God in a mysterious way. I have written this book to help people to pay attention to these encounters, to engage in a direct relationship with God, and to recognize some of the barriers to a more intimate relationship. As individuals and as church we need to pay attention to our experience in order to discern how God is leading us as individuals and as a community.

I hope this book will make prayer believable for ordinary people. And by opening up the issue of communal discernment in the church, it may help people to bring their actual experience of God to bear on some painful issues we face as a community.

Many people have found various articles I have published helpful for their prayer life. Since these articles are hard to come by, friends have suggested that I offer them as a book. Though hesitating to do so, I recently realized that a number of the articles reflected on a text of scripture or an idea about our relationship with God and described a deepening of that relationship. The action philosophy of Scottish philosopher John Macmurray and the spiritual theology of Sebastian Moore provided yet another line of continuity.

This book, then, consists of edited versions of the original articles and an indication of common themes and development. These meditations complement the thoughts on prayer contained in two earlier books, *God and You: Prayer as a Personal Relationship* and *"Seek My Face": Prayer as a Personal Relationship in Scripture* (Paulist Press).

My hope for this book is that readers may be helped to relate more intimately to God and to find God "a lot better than he's made out to be," as my mother put it one time in her lilting Irish brogue.

Acknowledgments

I want to express my gratitude to the many people who have graced my life by telling me about their experiences of God. I have dedicated this book to this, by now, rather large group of people. Each of them has a face and a name to me, but here they remain anonymous. They are, however, etched in my heart forever.

I want to thank by name people who have read my work and encouraged me to continue to publish: my father, William Barry, who at 91 still reads everything I write; my sisters, Peg, Mary and Kathleen; my cousins Madeline Shea, Mary McKendrick, Bill and Mary Shea, Tim and Hannah Devane, Kathleen Clifford, and Mary Burke; my friends Patricia Geoghegan, Philomena Sheerin, M.M.M., Joe McCormick, S.J., Jerry Calhoun, S.J., John and Denise Carmody, Bob Manning, S.J., and the Jesuit novices with whom I lived the past three years.

I am responsible for whatever of error may be contained in these pages; I believe in my heart that whatever of good is contained herein I owe, under God, to those who have loved me and encouraged me and trusted me with what is most precious to them, their hearts and the ground of those hearts, their God.

 *Part One*

Prayer as Personal Relationship

Many people today are looking for help with their prayer. First we will look at the foundation of prayer as a personal relationship and then at some blocks to developing a relationship with God. I hope to point out a way to enter more deeply into that relationship.

1

The Experience That Grounds Our Relationship

Almost anyone who has made an Ignatian retreat has heard of "The First Principle and Foundation." As it stands, near the beginning of Ignatius' *Spiritual Exercises*, it reads like the answer to the catechism question: "Why did God make me?"

> Man (sic) is created to praise, reverence, and serve God our Lord, and by this means to save his soul. The other things on the face of the earth are created for man to help him in attaining the end for which he is created. Hence, man is to make use of them insofar as they help him in the attainment of his end, and he must rid himself of them insofar as they prove a hindrance to him. Therefore, we must make ourselves indifferent to all created things, as far as we are allowed free choice and are not under any prohibition. Consequently, as far as we are concerned, we should not prefer health to sickness, riches to poverty, honor to dishonor, a long life to a short life. The same holds for all other things. Our one desire and choice should be what is more conducive to the end for which we are created.

As a doctrinal statement it is hard to fault. One might have to clarify what Ignatius means by "indifferent," but most Christians would assent to the statement's content. If, however, it remains for me a purely notional assent, it will hardly ground my life; it will not be *my* first principle and foundation.

16   PAYING ATTENTION TO GOD

Prayer is a conscious relationship with God. Since the central purpose of the *Spiritual Exercises* is the development of this conscious relationship, which cannot but have a profound effect on one's way of life, we can perhaps view the "first principle and foundation" as the grounding of our relationship with the Lord. As such it will have to be more than a doctrinal notion. Relationships develop only when there is an affective base. The first principle and foundation must be based on a loving encounter with the living God as well as upon doctrinal teaching. I want to draw out the personal and pastoral implications of this statement.

Relationships develop through mutual self-revelation. But I will only reveal myself to you if I trust you, if I believe that you will accept me as I am revealed to you. The foundation of any growing intimacy must be a trust that the other wants to know me, is positively inclined toward me. With greater reason, I believe, the foundation of a growing intimacy with God must be such trust. And it cannot be assumed that the achievement of such trust is readily available.

A number of years ago I discovered the following statement by British psychiatrist J. S. Mackenzie, cited and endorsed by the psychoanalyst Henry Guntrip (in *Psychotherapy and Religion*):

> The *enjoyment of God* should be the supreme end of spiritual technique; and it is in that enjoyment of God that we feel not only saved in the Evangelical sense, but safe: we are conscious of belonging to God, and hence are never alone; and, to the degree we have these two, hostile feelings disappear. . . . In that relationship Nature seems friendly and homely; even its vast spaces instead of eliciting a sense of terror speak of the infinite love; and the nearer beauty becomes the garment with which the Almighty clothes Himself.

Guntrip himself notes: "It is a common experience in psychotherapy to find patients who fear and hate God, a God who, in the words of J. S. Mackenzie, 'is always snooping around after sinners.'. . .'' Anyone who has done pastoral work can attest that this is a common experience among many Christians. And while sermons and homilies whose theme is the love of God may help, ultimately people need to experience that love. It will tax our ingenuity to develop the spiritual techniques or pastoral practices that will help people to have such a foundational experience.

It may help us with our own relationship to God and in pastoral practice if we can locate in our own experience those experiences which have been foundational. In my book *"Seek My Face"* I used Sebastian Moore's ideas from *Let This Mind Be in You* to suggest that all of us have experiences of a desire for "I know not what," a desire not for this or that lovely being (although the occasion for the experience may be the presence of some lovely being), but a desire for the unnameable, the "All," the Mystery we call God. I indicated that this experience could be seen as the experience of our own creation as someone desired into being by God. Let me repeat here the account of an experience I had that may spur the reader's own memories.

I was walking by the sea shore on a lovely, clear, crisp autumn day. I admired the sun on the leaves and on the blue water. Suddenly there welled up in me a feeling of great well-being and a strong desire for "I know not what," for the "All," for union, that made me very happy. I remembered a few other times of such joy and desire and realized why autumn is my favorite season—because it is associated with such experiences. Almost as quickly as it came it was gone. I was happy afterwards, not downcast even though I no longer had the experience. I would like to have the experience again, but I am not bereft without it. Later that week in a class I recounted the occasion, and many in the class acknowledged having similar experiences. I wonder if these are not experiences of our creation.

After all God is the only one who can directly touch the core of our desirableness. His desire makes us desirable, makes us "the apple of his eye." It would be strange indeed if we never experienced that core reality. In the experience I had there was, besides the desire for the "All," a sense of personal well-being. I felt good about myself insofar as I thought of myself at all. So it does not seem odd to think of the experience as an experience of my creation.

I believe that such an experience of our creation is the affective first principle and foundation upon which not only the Ignatian *Exercises* rest, but upon which any development of a personal relationship with God must rest. Only when I have at least some affective appreciation of the depth of God's love will I be willing and able to say and mean the final words of Psalm 139:

> Search me, O God, and know my heart;
> test me and know my anxious thoughts.
> See if there be any offensive way in me,
> and lead me in the way everlasting.

If I do not know in my bones that God loves me with an everlasting love, I will not dare to open myself to his gaze and to ask to see myself as he sees me. Even with a strong experience-based faith and trust in God's creative love for me I will still blanch before such a request. Yet my relationship with the Lord cannot develop unless I walk through this dark valley and come to know that the love that desired me into being still holds me as the apple of God's eye though I have been unfaithful and untrue, even outrageously so.

I want to draw out two implications of these reflections for pastoral practice. First, those of us who engage in any kind of pastoral ministry need to bend every effort to help people to have, or better, to pay attention to such foundational experiences. They are the "Abba" experiences which Jesus seemed so intent that people have. They are the foundation for a way of life which lets God become more and more the central relationship and the touchstone for all other relationships. Only when people believe in such a God and experience such a God will they be able to reform their lives in accordance with the demands of being true to that relationship.

Second, if it is possible for people to become aware of their creation, then such an experience may well be more widely available than we at present think. Much pastoral practice presumes that people need remedial pastoral care, psychotherapy, counseling, or the corporal works of mercy before they will be ready for the foundational experience of God. No doubt such spiritual and corporal works of mercy are not only helpful but needed, and surely called forth from Christians by their empathy for those in need. But God's creative love is touching people all the time, even in their moments of darkest pain. Perhaps, along with our merciful acts, we might also be alert to ways of helping people to experience that loving caress which even now makes them desirable as the apple of God's eye.

✺ 2 ✺
God's Freedom and Prayer

Once attracted into a relationship with God people are often hindered by certain images of God and by theological theories they have imbibed early in life. One of the more persistent hindrances may be detected in the following situations.

> The prayers of the faithful are about to conclude. People have prayed for physical healing of friends, for reconciliation in Northern Ireland, for people who are dying, for peace of mind for the mentally ill, and in their hearts for many personal gifts from God. The priest gathers all these needs into a final prayer: "God, grant us all these needs, but only if it is your will. You know what is best for us."

> During a spiritual direction session the director asks the directee what she desires of God. She is nonplussed and replies, "I never think in those terms. God is free and he knows what is best for me."

> A person experiences great dryness in prayer; God seems miles away. When he mentions this to his spiritual director, she points out that God sometimes distances himself, that the saints have often spoken of the dark night, etc. So he need not be troubled by the distance; God is sovereignly free and gives his graces as he wishes.

I suspect that many of us have had experiences like these. The basic theological axiom behind them is God's

sovereign freedom: God is not bound by anything or anyone outside himself. He cannot be coerced. He freely be-
stows his grace as he wishes. Since God is also goodness
and kindness itself, if he does not grant us our requests, it
must be because the granting of the request is not good for
us or for the person for whom we pray. Hence, many of us
either do not press our requests or hedge them around with
conditional phrases such as those of the priest at the end of
the prayers of the faithful. I believe that the theological axiom, true as it is, often is a hindrance to our growth in intimacy with God. Perhaps the following reflections will help.

It is true that God is sovereignly free and cannot be coerced by our desires. It need not follow, however, that we
should keep our desires to ourselves and wait for God's lar-
gesse or so temporize that only a God who can see through
the thicket of words can figure out what we really want.

Let us, for a moment, reflect on how friendships grow
in intimacy. The more of ourselves we reveal to another,
the more we develop intimacy. A close friend may intuit
what I feel or desire, but if I am hesitant to express my feelings or desires to him or her, we have a problem of intimacy. The issue is not one of knowledge, but of trust and
transparency. Intimacy requires growing transparency. I
let go of some of my defenses in order to let the other see me
as I am.

With regard to God, people often say, "There's no
need to tell him how I feel or what I desire because he
knows already." What is in question is not God's knowledge but my trust in him, my willingness to be as transparent as I can be before him. Do I *want* him to see me as I am? If
I wish to grow in intimacy with God, therefore, it may be
necessary that I tell him how I feel and what I really want—
not to increase his knowledge, but to draw closer to him.

Thus, the naked expression of what we really want
may be a necessary step toward intimacy. It may be that we
do not grow in intimacy with God because we cannot or do

not or will not tell him what we feel and desire. It has been
my experience that stiltedness and boredom in prayer are
often broken when a person can say that he is angry at God
for a loss or a suffering, that she is disappointed at not having a desire fulfilled, that he wants to experience God's
presence and is frustrated and angry at the felt distance.
What is at stake are not "answers" to life's difficulties or
more clarity about God's purposes, but intimacy.

A further reflection may help us. In human relationships we often add riders to our requests, but our purpose
is to make sure that the other does not feel coerced. Thus, I
might want to spend some time with a friend; at the same
time I do not want him to feel obliged to take the time. I
want him to *want* to be with me. In other words, I'm not
sure a) that my friend is free, and/or b) that he will be honest with me if he does not want to spend time right now,
and/or c) that he wants to be with me as much as I want to
be with him, and/or d) that I really want to be with him.

We all can recognize how convoluted communication
can get under these circumstances. Friendship can suffer as
a result. If we really believed that God is free, would we
have to reassure him on that point so often? It may be that
the reassurances stem from our own insecurities, our fears
that if we really ask him for what we want we will not get
it—and then we will feel rejected. Or again we may be ambivalent about our desires; we may, for example, both desire God's closeness and be terrified of him. Thus, the truism about God's sovereign freedom should actually lead us
to the naked expression of our desires; he cannot be coerced by them. We can ask straight out precisely because he
is free.

A third reflection follows from the second. God cannot
be coerced by anyone else. But what if God has bound himself? Again the relationship analogy is helpful. I am free to
commit myself to another person or not; but once I commit
myself to friendship or marriage or spiritual direction or

pastoral counseling, then I am bound by my word, my commitment. If I am to be a person of my word, then I will not lightly renege on my commitment.

If we take the Old and New Testaments seriously, God has freely committed himself to intimacy with us, an intimacy of parent to child, of lover to beloved, of friend to friend. One could read the Bible as a testament of God's dogged determination to convince us of the seriousness of *his* desire for a relationship of intimacy with us as a people and as individuals. Perhaps some of our problems in prayer stem from our unwillingness or inability to believe God. It may not be too whimsical to think of God as a frustrated lover who cannot seem to get through to us that he really does love us and want our intimate friendship.

Moreover, in the gospels Jesus is depicted as assuring us that God wants to answer our requests. In Luke, for instance, we read: "So I say to you: Ask and it will be given to you; seek and you will find; knock and the door will be opened to you. For everyone who asks receives; he who seeks finds; and to him who knocks, the doors will be opened" (Lk 11: 9-10). In one of his poems, French poet Charles Péguy has God the Father saying that his Son has made it impossible for him to see human beings in any other way than as sons and daughters; Péguy's God sounds like a bemused father whose hands are tied by love. Perhaps we need to take these words of Luke's gospel more seriously. The Our Father itself is a model of direct request with no ifs or buts: "Give us this day our daily bread."

It may be objected that the accounts of Jesus' agony in the garden have him put a rider onto his prayer. Luke's text reads like one of the prayers we used as initial examples: "Father, if you are willing, take this cup from me; yet not my will, but yours be done" (Lk 22: 42). But Mark's gospel has Jesus first ask directly for what he wants: "Abba, Father, everything is possible for you. Take this cup from me." Only then does Jesus add: "Yet not what I will, but

what you will'' (Mk 14: 36). The early church did not think
it out of character for Jesus at this critical juncture of his life
and of salvation history to ask directly that God take away
this suffering. That he could be depicted as voicing such a
desire seems almost a proof that we need not hedge on ex-
pressing any of our desires to God.

Let us return to the three examples at the beginning. It
would seem more trusting and more in keeping with the
promises of the gospels for the priest at the conclusion of
the prayers of the faithful to remind God of those promises
and to tell him that we make these petitions in hope and
trust because of the promises.

The woman in spiritual direction needs to be helped to
recognize that desires are a precondition for a fruitful experience of prayer, at least in an Ignatian retreat. Before each
period of prayer Ignatius advises the retreatant to ask for
what he or she wants. If retreatants have no desires, what
can they expect of God?

The person who experiences great dryness in prayer
does not need to be told about the dark night. He needs
help to express to God how this distance and dryness make
him feel and what he wants of God. Whatever coercion
God may experience is the coercion he has taken upon himself by freely committing himself to us as a people and as
individuals. If he does not want to answer our requests, he
will let us know that; we need not make excuses for him
prior to his decision.

3

Grief, Rage and Prayer

Over the years people have told me of experiences
similar to the following fictitious example:

My closest friend, Mary, was dying a long, painful,
wasting death. I was distraught and had nowhere to
turn. I tried to pray, asking God to relieve Mary of
her pain, but I felt that God was a million miles
away. One night the dam burst. I told God off in no
uncertain terms, even cursed him for what was happening to Mary. Then I cried until I thought there
could be no tears left. The strange thing was that
God seemed very close and comforting. The pain
was still there; in fact, it seemed even more intense.
Yet at the same time there was an intense feeling almost of joy. It was as if in spite of the pain Mary and
I were wrapped in love.

In this chapter I want to look more closely at such experiences to see what they tell us about God, life and
prayer. Often enough, when tragedy strikes, religious people either say to themselves, or hear said, statements such
as these: "God knows best what is good for us"; "Offer up
the suffering for the good of others"; "I'll keep you in my
prayers"; "Jesus will comfort you." Sometimes we wonder whether we are being punished for sins. And there are
"friends" such as Job had who will tell us that the latter is
probably the case or that we are being tested by God.
Truth to tell, all of us have a built in bias which social
psychologists have recently named the "just world hypothesis." In a just world the innocent do not suffer.

25

Hence, we tend to look for the cause of suffering in something the sufferer did. The rape victim, for example, "must have done something wrong." Either she was seductive or she went to the wrong part of town. "He got cancer because he bottled up his anger." People who are killed by mud slides from a volcano "should not have built so close to the mountain." Jesus himself heard a version of the just world hypothesis from his disciples: "Rabbi, who sinned, this man or his parents, that he was born blind?" (Jn 9:2). The just world hypothesis is so pervasive that even victims tend to blame themselves.

It is small wonder that this hypothesis holds such sway. In a world where tragedy falls randomly, I may be the next victim. Worse yet, there is no way to protect myself or those dearest to me. And finally, if the world is not just, then what kind of God created it? Indeed, if the world is not just, is there a God? Is there *any* meaning in life? Such thoughts can cause great anxiety. Thus, there are powerful motives for holding adamantly to the just world hypothesis.

Yet the book of Job seems to have been written precisely to belie that theory. Neither Job nor his family deserved the suffering they underwent. In John 9:3 Jesus denies the premise of the disciples about the man born blind: "Neither this man nor his parents sinned, but this happened so that the work of God might be displayed in his life." This statement, however, compounds the problem because it seems to make God responsible for the pain the man born blind and his parents have suffered. At the same time, if we take the statement seriously and without recourse to exegetical and theological explanations, we may gain some insight into the dilemma forced on us by the rejection of the just world hypothesis.

What is our inner reaction when we hear stories of the unjust treatment of others or even more when we are the object of what seems to us unjust treatment? Are we not filled with anger, resentment, even rage? For all my desires to be a pacifist, for example, I can feel murderous anger rising in me when I watch a movie depicting injustice against innocent people. Now let us imagine that someone has perfected a cure for blindness, but needs a blind person to use it on. So he picks out a baby and blinds it and later offers the cure. It sounds horrible and perverse, does it not? But yet, this is one interpretation of Jesus' words about the man born blind. I wonder how many of us have suppressed the thought that Jesus meant something like that. And if we have ever taken seriously the opening chapter of the book of Job, then we must have felt a flaring up of resentment at the way Job is tossed to Satan by God. But, of course, most of us quickly resort to ''better'' thoughts about God. ''That is not what Jesus meant. Scripture scholars must be able to explain the passage in John.'' ''The story in Job is just that, an anthropomorphic way for the writer to make his point.''

But if God is love and all-powerful, as we have been taught since childhood, why does he let horrors such as children being born blind happen?—the age-old question of theodicy, perhaps never put so strongly as in the story of the Grand Inquisitor in *The Brothers Karamazov*. I do not believe that for most of us the question is answered satisfactorily by philosophy or theology. And I suspect that many of us are prevented from a closer relationship to God by the suppression of anger and resentment at life's sufferings or of the anxiety that rises when we begin to question the just world hypothesis.

Let us look more closely at the example with which I began this reflection, a fictitious example, to be sure, but one that captures the essence of the experiences described by many people who confided in me. ''I felt that God was a million miles away.'' This experience of God's distance came before the bursting of the dam. I venture to say that the feeling of distance was due to the suppression of the rage at God or of the questions about God's goodness, love, or concern.

Elizabeth Kübler-Ross says that a period of rage and resentment is part of the process of grieving and facing death. As noted earlier, a natural reaction to injustice is rage and the desire to retaliate. That reaction must very often be against the seeming injustices life visits upon us and thus against the Author of life.

We know what happens in a close relationship when one party gets very angry at the other because of a real or apparent injustice but suppresses the expression of the anger because of fear of the loss of the relationship or for some other reason. Conversations between them grow more polite and bland because to touch on serious issues would require opening up the raw wound. The injured party may harbor hopes that the other will notice that something is wrong and beg forgiveness. If the two people are lucky, the injured party gradually loses sight of the grievance, and they begin to share at deeper levels. But the unhealed wound may fester and be opened up again by a chance remark. The relationship may never move to the deeper levels that seemed possible before the injury. Because the injured party did not want to risk losing "everything," i.e., the whole relationship, the relationship may be doomed to stagnation.

The same dynamic often operates in our relationship with God, that is, in our prayer. The suppression of anger or rage at God or of anxiety about the justice and meaning of life may create a gulf between us and God in our experience. He may seem "a million miles away" just when we need him most. Our prayers to God become perfunctory and ritualistic, much as with a friend who has hurt us conversation tends to be about the weather or other banalities. Words are used to fill up the time. With God we may rationalize the experience of distance with ideas about God's sovereign freedom, about his difference from us, or about the "dark night" as a testing ground. We forget that the saints were able to tell God that they did not like the way he seemed to be treating them. Even if it is the dark night sent by God to purify me, I may not like it and, if I trust God, can tell him so. Ultimately, what keeps us from being honest with our human friends as well as with God is our fear that honesty will destroy the relationship. No wonder God seems ''a million miles away.''

Now notice what happened ''when the dam burst.'' The rage spilled out. I have known people who cursed and swore at God, some who felt that they were handing him back their entrance ticket to the universe, as it were. It really was explosive, like a dam bursting. And yet they did not find themselves totally alienated and lost. They felt, at the least, relieved that they had finally told the truth and that God had listened. Some have felt a deep compassion embracing them in their pain as though they had been striking in rage at a parent who not only did not strike back, but held on to them with love and care. These people have come to a deep realization that, for all its pain and suffering, life really is about love, and the universe is a ''homely'' place.

Scottish philosopher John Macmurray has this wonderful saying:

> The maxim of illusory religion runs: ''Fear not; trust in God and He will see that none of the things you fear will happen to you''; that of real religion, on the contrary, is: ''Fear not; the things that you are afraid of are quite likely to happen to you, but they are nothing to be afraid of'' (Gifford Lectures, 1953-54).

What these people who poured out their honest feelings to God came to experience is that in spite of the pain—and sometimes the pain is intensified by the experience of God's presence to it—there is nothing to be afraid of. Darkness and light, pain and joy, death and resurrection are fused, are one experience, and darkness, pain and death do not triumph.

Moreover, they have entered into a more intimate relationship with God. Their prayer life changes, and for the better. Now they know that God really does embrace their darkness as well their light, their rage as well as their love. They have been as transparent before God as they could be and God has not only accepted them, but embraced them. "If God can still love me when he knows how much hatred I harbored toward him, then I can tell him anything." Prayer then becomes a real dialogue.

And dialogue means that God too communicates. What does God reveal of himself? At the least, that he understands and is compassionate, that he really does love us beyond our imagination to predict. But I have often felt that he reveals even more. In these moments of shared pain and rage and grief, there can come over us a sense of an enormous sob, as if the Creator himself were crying out: "This is not what I intended!" An anthropomorphic projection, one might say. But all our affirmations about God are anthropomorphic. The only way human beings can receive God's revelation of himself is through human minds and hearts and viscera. Even Jesus could express who God was only through his humanity. So perhaps in these moments of shared grief we do learn about God; indeed, it is only by engaging in the relationship at deeper and deeper levels that we will ever "know" who God really is.

If we understand prayer as personal relationship and follow through on the consequences of that definition, then we will find that strong emotions, even strongly negative or painful emotions, are not foreign to prayer. Indeed, they are the stuff of prayer as they are of any relationship. Just as we human beings do not know how deep our trust and love of one another is until we open up our dark sides, so too we will not know how deep the mutual love and trust is between God and us until we let him see us as we are. Only then, too, will we know that death and resurrection are one experience.

⨌ 4 ⨌

Resistance to Union:
A Virulent Strain

The next three chapters take up some aspects of our ambivalence toward a more intimate relationship with the Lord. In one way or another they discuss resistance to positive experiences of God.

Usually when we think about resistance to a deeper intimacy with the Lord, the issues revolve around the avoidance of pain. A man is afraid that he will be punished for his sins if he gets too close to God. Or a woman avoids a more personal relationship with the Lord because she fears the demands that might be made on her to change her lifestyle. St. Ignatius seems to bear out this line of reasoning in his rules for the discernment of spirits. For those who are advancing in the way of perfection, he says, ''. . .it is characteristic of the evil spirit to harass with anxiety, to afflict with sadness, to raise obstacles backed by fallacious reasonings that disturb the soul.'' A phenomenon not often marked in books on prayer is a resistance that seems to be based on the avoidance of a pleasurable experience of God, some type of unitive experience.

For a few years I have been intrigued by something that happened to me. I was on sabbatical and spending much of my time alone at a beach house, writing. For about ten years prior to this year I had been very active, indeed overactive, in exciting and satisfying apostolic work. So the year gave me more time for prayer and reflection. But the period during this year that I want to talk about was not so tranquil.

I had just spent three weeks in Jamaica directing retreats and supervising the beginning of a center for training spiritual directors and then returned to the beach house for a couple of weeks. I felt beset by personal fears and anxiety. I made an Intensive Journal workshop one weekend around this time during which I prayed for a deeper trust in God and a wholehearted love for him and his people. My notes from that weekend indicate that I did experience a growing clarity of focus in my life and a deepening sense of the Lord's presence and attractiveness. I do not recall much about the next couple of weeks, but I do have a rather vivid memory of a two-week period which included a trip to Dallas to participate in an intensive five-day workshop. During this period I was in what I can only describe as "the flow." As I look back on it, it seems that I was aware of God's presence very often. Periodically I would realize that the atmosphere in a group or with an individual was charged with a Presence that was palpable. I often found myself commending people I was with to God and yet I was very present to them.

Others felt something different but good in my presence. I seemed able to do things easily and quickly that ordinarily would have taken much more time and energy. I was not fretting about the past or the future but could be present to this task now. I could love without clutching on, and I could write freely and easily. It was a period, as I remember it, when I was able to follow the old axiom, *Age quod agis* (Do what you are doing) at most moments, and I could be alone easily and joyfully as well.

But something happened to pull me out of the flow, and I do not know what it was. What is more surprising, I did not notice the change or try to find out what had happened, nor have I been able in the ensuing years to ask the Lord with all my heart for such wholeheartedness again. One would think that I would be hankering for it continually. It looks to me like a massive resistance, but for the life of me I cannot recall that the experience was painful, at least no more painful than life can be at any time. In fact, my recollection is that the time was exciting, alive and rather more joyful than usual.

In the intervening years I have periodically run into people who seem to have had similar experiences. That is, they speak about very positive religious experiences which are followed inexplicably by periods of avoiding prayer, and they are puzzled by the sequence. In one instance, a person on retreat told me of four periods of prayer in one day which were very heart-warming and moving as he felt how much the Lord loved him and enjoyed his company. The next day of retreat he decided that he had better use the prayer times to make plans for his apostolic work after retreat. It was only when we looked at how his prayer had shifted that he realized that he was running away from the positive experience of the day before.

Such experiences seem to occur to people who are serious enough about the spiritual life and their relationship with the Lord to pray regularly and see a spiritual director. In other words, they are not neophytes in prayer. I began to formulate the idea that something in us could not brook too much intimacy with God. As a spiritual director I helped people to notice the ambivalence and to ask the Lord's help to overcome it. (I was slow to follow the advice myself, however.)

This strain of resistance seemed especially hardy, and I began to wonder about its source. Indeed, the strain seemed so strong, so adamantine that I was reminded of the shout attributed to Lucifer, "I will not serve!" and considered that the evil one might be at least one source, if not the main culprit. I also felt that the source might be that part of us that cannot let God be the only God because we want to be in control. One rather thick strand of the scriptural tapestry seems to be God's continual attempts to prove to us humans that he, Mystery itself, the Holy One, is really benign, really to be trusted, only to find us radically unwilling or unable to believe him because to do so means to give up the illusion of control of our lives.

Gerald May's book, *Care of Mind, Care of Spirit*, gave me a clue. At one point he quotes a directee who is puzzled that he has pulled away from a very positive experience of God. Instead of looking at such behavior as just another instance of neurosis, May notes that "the directee is struggling with the very existence of self-image in the face of close appreciation of the divine." Later in the book he says: "Ironically, one may have great trouble praying after going through an especially beautiful, consoling experience. Such experiences often imply considerable unconscious threat to self-importance in spite of their overt beauty. One's reaction to this may sometimes be to turn away from prayer for a while, and one may be mystified as to the reason."

In an earlier article May notes the "deep threat and anxiety" which spiritual experience engenders. "Spiritual experience becomes even more threatening if it is viewed as an accurate perception of the-way-things-are rather than some kind of isolated 'high.' Specifically, when one is in the midst of such experience, one cannot be in the business of defining oneself. . . . One's ego, sense of identity, self-image seem to evaporate almost magically. And one is left, just simply being." From the deep levels of our being, he believes, anxiety begins to rise, and we defend ourselves by running away from the experience and even repressing the memory of it.

Could this be it then, that what we most deeply yearn for we most deeply fear? When we are united with God, we see reality whole, and we are not the center of it. This "vision" is deeply gratifying and reassuring at one level and deeply threatening at another. Moreover, we fear the loss of self in surrendering to God, and this even though our continual experience of encounters with God indicates the paradoxical opposite: that the closer we are united with God the more ourselves we are. The patriarchs and prophets of Israel discovered this paradoxical truth, Jesus carried the experience to its zenith, and holy women and men down through the ages have witnessed to the same truth. We ourselves have had inklings of the truth in our experience. Nevertheless, despite all the evidence, we continually back off as if from a precipice over an abyss.

What can we do about this virulent strain of resistance? It is easy enough to shout to someone else: "You have nothing to lose but your chains, or your blinders," but what can we do with ourselves? First, it is a great help to have a spiritual director, because it is the nature of this resistance to make us blind to the problem. In fact, at the time of my own experience I was not seeing a spiritual director with any regularity and thus was able to avoid paying close attention to the shift that occurred. Even if one has a director, the problem can be missed because one does not talk about the positive experience and its sequel of resistance. Spiritual directors might be alerted to the possibility of the presence of this strain of resistance by the realization that spiritual experience, i.e., the experience of God, seems readily available to anyone who wants it. Thus, if a directee who desires God's presence does not experience God over a lengthy period of time, it might be prudent to look back to the last period of alive prayer to see what happened before one too quickly thought of the dark night of the soul. Not that there is no such phenomenon as the dark night; rather it should not be too easily presumed to be present before all other avenues have been pursued.

Let's suppose that with the help of a director one has unearthed this kind of resistance. What can one do now? It seems so much a part of the human condition to fear what one most wants, namely union with God, that one despairs of overcoming the resistance. We can become dismayed at the impossibility of the task, just as the alcoholic is dismayed at the thought of never having another drink.

Perhaps we can take a leaf from the Alcoholics Anonymous program which encourages the alcoholic to take one day, one hour, one step at a time and to admit to God one's helplessness to save oneself. We express to God our profound desire to encounter and trust him and our almost as profound fear of doing so and ask his help to overcome our ambivalence—and keep overcoming it.

Moreover, we need to keep reminding ourselves that as long as we are alive, this strain of resistance will also be alive. I am reminded of the chicken pox virus which lodges in a nerve cell of the spinal column after the disease has run its course. At any moment it can break out in the very irritating and painful rash called shingles. There is nothing one can do to get rid of the virus strain. So too with the strain of resistance described here. No wonder that saints could realize how deeply sinful they were, the closer they came to God. But remember: "The light shines in the darkness, and the darkness has not overcome it" (Jn 1:5).

⤜ 5 ⤚

The Desire to Love as Jesus Loved: Its Vicissitudes

In the last chapter we discussed the resistance to unitive experiences of God which comes over people who have a rather well-developed conscious relationship with the Lord. There we noted that the experience of the Lord that is being resisted or avoided is a very positive one, and we speculated on the reasons for the resistance. Now I want to look at a similar phenomenon, but from a slightly different angle. I believe that I can be less speculative and more experiential about the reasons for this resistance.

At some point in many people's developing relationship with the Lord, companionship with Jesus becomes the focus. He has been experienced as their savior, the one who died for their sins, the one who loves them and every human being in spite of all that we do to injure him and one another. And his love is transforming; it enables them to turn over a new leaf, to ask for forgiveness, to repent and believe the good news. They then desire to know Jesus better, to love him more, and to follow him, as Ignatius of Loyola formulates the desire of the Second Week of his *Spiritual Exercises*. The phenomenon I want to examine more closely seems to occur when this process of getting to know and love Jesus is well advanced. People begin to want to love as Jesus loves. We will try to follow the vicissitudes of this desire.

After the conversion experience of accepting the Lord's forgiving love people generally realize that the ac-

ceptance of such forgiveness pushes them to ask for the
grace to forgive those who have hurt them. Thus they already desire to love as Jesus loves. But as they get to know
Jesus better through the contemplation of the gospels, they
notice that Jesus gets precious little return on his invest-
ment of love and yet he keeps on loving. Perhaps the clear-
est examples occur as the storm clouds that eventually pre-
cipitate his death begin to loom more ominously. Between
chapters 8 and 10 of Mark's gospel Jesus three times predicts his passion and three times his chosen companions,
his closest friends, badly miss the point. After the first pre-
diction Peter tries to tell him it will not happen; after the
second the companions argue about who will be number
one, and after the third James and John ask to sit at his right
and his left. What people notice after a while is that Jesus
continues to love these friends of his and continues to love
the people who are eventually going to demand his death,
as he continues to love Judas, his betrayer. They realize that
Jesus even loves the religious leaders who oppose him; his
anger at them does not block out his love.

To those who are developing their companionship
with Jesus these are heady realizations. At first they may be
elated that they are privileged to know the heart of Jesus at
such depth. They may ask to be able to love as he does and
may imagine some ways of carrying it off. Often enough
their images are of doing something heroic out of love, for
example, of leaving one's present, relatively secure posi-
tion and home for work with the poor in a foreign country.
When they look at the meditation on the three kinds of hu-
mility in the *Spiritual Exercises*, as another example, they
may find themselves desiring ''poverty with Christ poor,
rather than riches; insults with Christ loaded with them,
rather than honors; . . . to be accounted as worthless and a
fool for Christ. . . .'' They may note some hesitation or even
repugnance to making such desires known to the Lord and
to imagining themselves in a foreign land, but these are

taken as normal reactions and not as serious obstacles to continuing to follow Jesus and become like him. Intellectually they know their limitations as human beings, but they also know intellectually that God's grace can move mountains.

Then something happens to bring home how firmly and deeply rooted the mountain really is. One man on a 30-day retreat became obsessed by the "thoughtlessness" of a close friend and with the help of his director realized how far he was from really desiring to love as Jesus loved. A woman who had earlier dreamed of living and working with the poor in a dangerous area found herself unable and unwilling to forgive one of her co-workers until the other said she was sorry. A person on retreat begins to imagine in the concrete what it would be like back home to love as Jesus loves, and balks at it because there would be no credit, e.g., "They will not understand how changed I am and why." Usually the "something" that happens is close to home and pops the balloon of self-inflation that dreams of doing great exploits for far-away people.

When something concrete like this happens, prayer can come to a grinding halt. The "thoughtless" friend becomes the central focus, for instance, and the person begins to fret about what to do to make the friend shape up. Or the person may become desolate about his or her shortcomings and begin to think that nothing has really changed after all this commitment to prayer. Or the desire to love as Jesus loves is seen as illusory, a form of megalomania that deserves its comeuppance. In these and other ways the person praying takes his or her eyes off the Lord and focuses on self or someone else. If the focus is on someone else, it is mostly about how the other needs to change; interestingly enough, I can do nothing to change the other, but I focus my attention on that. If the focus is on the self, it usually revolves around how impossible it is for me to change, to become like Jesus, which, of course, is absolutely true, but irrelevant. One person, in fact, said to Jesus: "But I can't do it," and felt that his comeback was: "Of course you can't; whoever said you could?" The implication, she knew, was that she could, if she wanted to, ask God to do what she could not do. Success at loving as Jesus loves was not the issue, only the willingness to ask God's help.

Of course, at this point that is precisely the rub. What has surfaced is a repugnance even to want to love that way, to want to love without being sure of a return, to want to love, indeed, even where no comparable return is possible. When we imagine loving in that way, we seem to be facing the question of whether God is sufficient for us. Since this is, I believe, the unnerving question that sets off a massive resistance, I want to look carefully at it because its centrality at this point can easily be missed.

In spite of Carl Rogers' urging that parents give unconditioned love to their children, such unconditioned love is not in their or our power. Only God can of himself love unconditionally, and only God can empower human beings to love unconditionally. So we all grow up in an atmosphere of conditioned love. We expect to earn love by being or acting a certain way, and we give love just as conditionally. We reward those who are good to us and want to punish those who are not. We expect to be rewarded for being kind or generous, at least rewarded with gratitude or affection or a good name. Indeed, we are deeply offended when our "good deeds" are not so rewarded or are misunderstood. We know no other way of being until we meet someone who seems to love unconditionally, and even then we suspect some ulterior motive. This is ultimately why we find it so difficult to believe that God really does love us first, i.e., without first demanding that we shape up. We have precious little experience of receiving without having done something to deserve it or without being expected to do something in return.

Even after we have come to believe, at least partly and some of the time, in God's unconditioned love, we face a new and perhaps stronger resistance when the desire to love as Jesus loves takes strong root in our hearts. Jesus, after all, loves as God loves, unconditionally. Hence, it seems, he does not expect a return. God alone is his portion. Can we live this way? Something akin to terror strikes the heart. To desire to love as Jesus loves seems to mean to desire to be alone with the Alone, to want no recompense except God. There is a temptation here that is very subtly hidden in a kernel of truth. To see where it resides, let me be concrete, using a fictitious example that is a composite of many experiences.

Joe is a 45-year-old religious who teaches high school and lives with 15 other religious. On his sabbatical he makes a 30-day directed retreat and is at the point we are discussing. When the desire to love as Jesus loves first rises to consciousness, Joe is strongly moved to volunteer for a dangerous mission his order carries on in Central America. He imagines himself giving up everything to live and work with the downtrodden. He feels certain fears, but these do not hinder him from offering himself to the Lord. While out walking he imagines himself walking along with Jesus and the disciples as Jesus predicts his passion. He feels very close to Jesus and the disciples and senses how much Jesus loves them and him. Jesus knows their limitations and weaknesses, but really wants their companionship and friendship. Joe is reminded of his best friends in the order and how much he enjoys their company. Joe tells Jesus that he wants to love as he does and to suffer with him in Central America. The prayer period leaves him elated though somewhat uneasy.

The next time he prays he returns to the same scene. This time the quarreling among the disciples about the top spot catches his attention, and he feels angry at them and sorry for Jesus. His own friends come to mind, but now he feels some resentment toward them. They like to get together with Joe, but he has to do all the initiating and call-

ing; they never seem to call him spontaneously, or at least
not often. He cannot shake off the resentment; in fact, as he
reflects on the prayer period afterwards, he notes that once
the resentment about his friends surfaced he hardly paid
any attention to Jesus. He engaged in a number of imagi-
nary talks with his friends or with himself which circled
around his resentment. Even now the thoughts keep pes-
tering him. "Maybe they would just as soon get together
without me." "Well, Jesus didn't get much from his so-
called friends, either." "If I just keep initiating, am I not
treating them as somehow beneath me?" "Doesn't friendship mean mutuality?" These and other thoughts run
through his mind. Then he recalls that he had asked to be
able to love as Jesus loves and says to himself: "This is what
it means, then, that I keep on with my friends and just not
expect any reciprocity. Jesus died alone and friendless, depending only on God. That's what God wants of me. It
seems awfully lonely, but if that's what it takes to love as
Jesus loves, I won't renege on what I promised earlier. After all, when we die, we must willy-nilly trust in God
alone."

Joe tells his director about the day and his insight into
what it means to love as Jesus loves. The director notices
that Joe's voice is excited and even light-hearted as he
speaks of the first period of prayer but becomes rather grim
and determined when he describes the second, especially
when he tells about his insight. The director also notes that
in describing his second period of prayer and its aftermath
Joe has not once mentioned talking to Jesus or asking Jesus
how he felt toward his "friends." She gently points out her
perceptions and asks Joe how he feels about loving as Jesus
loves. As he talks, he becomes more and more resentful of
his situation. "If I do continue to intitiate our contacts, they
won't even notice. And I'll go down to Central America
and no one will give a rap." He remembers that he felt angry that God seemed to demand so much from Jesus and

now from him. He is no longer so sure that he wants to love as Jesus loves.

What is happening here? First of all, Joe has fallen into a scenario where he is being asked to be a "hero." There is something heroic about volunteering for Central America, and at one level Joe basks in the expected credit his action would receive in his order. Moreover, when he imagines himself in Central America, he is the giver; he has no thought of receiving anything from the people. In other words, Joe's motivation is not as straightforward as he believes. This is nothing to wonder at; after all Joe is just human. The Lord always has to draw us forward by way of tangled motivation. The purification of motives comes in the process.

Here the process leads to the seemingly trivial incident of Joe's resentment at his friends. Given the enormity of the world's problems and the really serious difficulties people face, Joe can seem to be fiddling while Rome burns. Yet of such trivialities is our real spiritual life made. Even here Joe is seeing himself in a "hero" role. Notice how he now interprets Jesus' relationship with his disciples. They are not "real" friends; Jesus gets nothing from his association with them. And Joe now interprets his own friendships in the same way and sees himself being asked to continue to give to them. He and Jesus are the lonely "heroes" who give without counting the cost and who expect nothing from anyone except God.

There is a kernel of truth in Joe's view. Jesus does love as God loves, unconditionally, and he does count ultimately only on the Father. But this does not mean that he does not receive something from those he loves. All it means is that the return is not the condition for the gift. After all, Jesus does call his disciples friends, and at the Last Supper at that. Moreover, some of his friends and his mother stayed with him to the bitter end. Jesus has been and is loved by many people throughout the history of

Christendom, and this is a return for his unconditional love. So too Joe forgets that he enjoys the company of his friends; he knows that they really do love him and appreciate him. Before the resentment rose, in fact, Joe had associated them with himself and the disciples around Jesus and felt how happy Jesus was to have them all as companions. To want to love as Jesus loves does mean to desire to love without putting conditions on the gift of love. In Joe's case it means the willingness to keep on initiating contacts with his friends or to talk honestly with them about his resentment, or at least the willingness to ask for the grace to be able to love in this way. The delusion is to think that to love as Jesus loves means to receive no human love at all in return. Perhaps one will be abandoned by all one's friends if one does become like Jesus, but it is not guaranteed. To believe that it is guaranteed is delusion. Here we have, I believe, a clear example of what Ignatius calls the evil spirit assuming "the appearance of an angel of light."

Even when Joe is helped to see what is happening in him, it may still not be easy for him to ask for the grace to love as Jesus loves. He may still balk at the lack of a guaranteed *quid pro quo.* He may still resent the "unselfishness" he is called to. What he needs help to do is to hang in there and not get discouraged or down on himself. Here is where the Ignatian idea of asking for the desire is very helpful. Even if he is too ambivalent to desire to love as Jesus loves, he may be able to ask Jesus to enkindle the desire in him, to purify his motives a bit more, to help him to know how Jesus was able to live his life so purposefully and fully.

One of the temptations at this point is to become almost despairing of ever changing. Joe can see that he has been happier, more fulfilled, more alive when he has been enabled to come close to loving as Jesus loves, and so he can find it almost diabolical that he cannot bring himself to ask wholeheartedly for the grace to love that way. It is a paradox, as I noted in the last chapter, that what is resisted is something that has been experienced as good. We can help Joe (and the Joe in each of us) by keeping a sense of humor about the paradoxes of human motivation and especially about the seeming inanities that surface whenever we humans allow God to get close. It seems that like Jerusalem we do not know what is for our peace even while at the same time we do know.

Let's end the story and the chapter. Finally, through the grace of God and his own perseverance, Joe is able to ask God to free him to want to love as Jesus loves. He then finds himself desiring to love as Jesus loves, and a great weight is lifted from his heart. Once again he can contemplate Jesus. Now he sees that Jesus often cares for the marginal people right in his midst, and Joe feels drawn to the students who are least responsive and perhaps most needy of attention. Jesus speaks the truth in season and out, and Joe finds himself raising the tough questions in his community that every religious community tries to skirt, e.g., questions about the quality of their religious and apostolic life together.

Joe may be a less than comfortable companion after this retreat. Once Joe or anyone asks to love as Jesus loves and more or less means it, the genie is out the bottle. Joe may yet end up in Central America, but if he does, he will go there not as a conquering hero but as a servant who hopes to be a sacrament of God's presence and who also hopes to find people who will be sacraments for him.

ଔଞ 6 ନ୍ତ

Surrender: The Key to Wholeness

In the last two chapters we have discussed a peculiar sort of resistance to God, a resistance that seems to be the avoidance of good experiences. Once in a prayer group discussion I received some more light on this puzzling phenomenon; I invite the reader's reflection with me.

Have you ever wondered about people like Bartimaeus, the blind beggar who receives his sight (Mk 10:46-51)? Did it ever occur to you that they might not want to be healed? Well it has occurred to me because there have been times when I have not wanted inner healing, the healing of resentment at a personal loss, for example. As a result I have thought that people like Bartimaeus have a rather remarkable kind of courage and hope in the future to want to be healed.

Let us reflect on what it must have meant for Bartimaeus as he pondered the question Jesus put to him, "What do you want me to do for you?" If he allows himself to want his sight, two possibilities open up. His hopes could be dashed as it proves impossible for Jesus to fulfill his desires. Often enough, I believe, we limit our desires precisely so that we will not be too disappointed. On the other hand, he could actually receive his sight. But what then? After all, he now has an identity that revolves around being a blind beggar. Who will he be if he is no longer blind? Moreover, he knows how to cope with who he now is. He makes a living and he gets attention and perhaps even pity from others. How will he live as a sighted person? Suppose that a great deal of his vital energy is fueled by resentment of the trick life has played on him. What will it be like not to have that resentment? His friends will have to learn new ways of dealing with him as well. Indeed, they may not be willing or able to make the transition to relating to a man who is no longer handicapped.

All of this may seem quite fanciful. Yet any counselor or spiritual director can testify that there is in us some power that is inherently conservative, that wants the *status quo* to be preserved no matter how painful it is. I may be between a rock and a hard place, but it is *my* rock and *my* hard place, and I know how to cope with the situation. Leaving it is very difficult, no matter how painful it also is to stay. Can we make sense of this difficulty of even desiring a change to something better?

I have already pointed to one source of the difficulty. My identity can be wrapped up in my present status whether that status is blind beggar, jilted lover, bereaved husband, unloved child, unappreciated co-worker, or whatever. To give up the identity may seem like giving up one's only self.

Moreover, as indicated earlier, I have built up around this identity ways of coping with life and even of earning a living. To change means to face an unknown, and perhaps worse, future.

There is, perhaps, a more subtle source of the resistance as well. Freudian analysts speak of the covert gratification neurotic symptoms bring to the one who has them. There can be covert sexual and/or aggressive gratification, for example, in a wife's agoraphobia (fear of open spaces) because her husband has to stay at home more with her and also has to do the shopping. Suicidal people have been known to get gratification from the thought of making others guilty, miserable, even sick by their own deaths. It may be that all of the *status quo*s which we find so hard to give up provide some covert gratification. For example, Bartimaeus might well wonder whether anyone will pay attention to him if he is no longer blind. Again, to want to be healed of the resentment caused by a friend's hurtful remarks may mean that I will have to give up the covert hope that my friend is feeling pangs of remorse.

We come close to the central insight I received at the prayer group. To want to be healed, to be changed, to become more whole means to surrender to life and to the future. The surrender involves two distinct, but interrelated movements, I believe. On the one hand, it means accepting my past as precisely what it is, *my past*. On the other hand, it means surrendering myself to the mystery of the future, ultimately to the Mystery we call God. We will look at each of these movements in turn.

Bartimaeus must have accepted his past. He is a blind man, a blind beggar. He does not seem to wallow in resentment at what life has done to him; if he did, he would not have been able to ask so forcibly for his sight. To come to this point of acceptance he may have had to go through all the stages of grief described so well by Elizabeth Kubler-Ross in *On Death and Dying*. He may have denied his blindness, raged at it, at life, and at God, bargained with God, and become depressed. But now he has accepted that he is blind. And yet it is accepted as somehow *past*, as not controlling his freedom now, his freedom to desire a change. "Rabbi, I want to see."

It is important to grasp the full impact of what it means for Bartimaeus or anyone of us to accept the past. It does not mean a stoic impassivity toward life. It does not mean a rosy optimism either. Life has dealt Bartimaeus a cruel blow, as it has dealt cruel blows to many people. Children have been subjected to abusive, unloving and unskilled parenting and have been psychically and spiritually scarred as a result. Loved ones have tragically and permanently been parted, and the survivors are wounded deeply. To accept the past does not mean to condone everyone and everything. But it does mean to forgive in some deep way.

Søren Kierkegaard makes a powerful statement while commenting on the biblical book of Tobit. Recall that Sarah has become a mockery to her own maid because seven men have died on their marriage night to her. Now Tobias has asked to marry her. Many see Tobias as the hero. ''No,'' says Kierkegaard,

> it is Sarah that is the heroine. . . . For what love of God it requires to be willing to let oneself be healed when from the beginning one has been thus bungled without one's fault, from the beginning has been an abortive specimen of humanity! What ethical maturity was required for assuming the responsibility of allowing the loved one to do such a daring deed! What humility before the face of another person! What faith in God to believe that the next instant she would not hate the husband to whom she owed everything! (*Fear and Trembling*).

To accept the past as *my* past brings a freedom from it. But the freedom does not mean that I am no longer the person that past has made me. Bartimaeus is who he is because he was a blind beggar. So, too, Sarah is who she is because of her history of marriages. Another example is supplied by Robert and Suzanne Massie's 20-year-old son who was born as a hemophiliac; at any moment of his life he could bleed to death from a simple cut. He was asked whether he wished that he had not had the illness. ''How can I—or anyone—wish that the most important thing that ever happened to me had not happened? It is like saying that I wish I had been born on another planet, so different would I probably be. Put it this way: I would not have it any other way'' (*Journey*).

And yet with this acceptance there comes a freedom from the past. Bartimaeus is free of the imprisoning identity ''blind beggar.'' Even if he does not receive his sight, he is free to become blind Bartimaeus the poet, or blind Barti-

maeus the husband of Mary, or blind Bartimaeus the fol-
lower of Jesus. Just as the young hemophiliac can, by accepting his past, become a doctor, a teacher, a husband
who also happens to be hemophiliac. To accept the past as
my past means to accept a future limited by my past, but
nonetheless a future.

Erik Erikson calls his final developmental stage the crisis between ego integrity and despair. Ego integrity or wisdom is described in *Childhood and Society*: "It is the acceptance of one's one and only life cycle as something that had
to be and that, by necessity, permitted of no substitutions:
it thus means a new, a different love of one's parents."
Such wisdom, Erikson maintains, leads to freedom from
the inordinate fear of death. And this may be the crux of the
resistance to accepting my past. Each such acceptance
means facing my mortality, my finitude, my limited existence. Much of our waking life is given over to avoiding that
reality. Small wonder that we resist acceptance of the past
as my past.

The second movement is precisely the surrender to the
mystery of the future. When Bartimaeus opens his heart to
desire sight, he opens himself to the unknown. He hands
himself over in faith and hope to the Lord of the future.
Mark's gospel gives some indication that the future may
not be very rosy. The story ends: "Immediately he received
his sight and followed Jesus along the road." The road here
is the way of the cross because the very next passage is the
triumphal entry into Jerusalem which begins Jesus' last
week of life. Kierkegaard's last comment about Sarah pin-
points the nature of the surrender. He says that she had to
have great faith in God to let Tobias risk his life for her. If
they did get through their wedding night, she would owe
him everything. Suppose that she then were to come to
hate him to whom she owed everything? The future she
had to trust to God. It is extremely difficult to do so. It can
seem like stepping off a cliff or jumping out of a boat expect-

ing to walk on air or water. The air may at first be bracing in one's new found trust and hope, but the landmarks are unfamiliar, the usual signposts missing. Like the Israelites in the desert we can hanker for the leeks and onions of Egypt. Like Peter on the water we can become afraid of the mysterious world we have entered. But we, too, can hear the Lord calling us to trust him, to keep on surrendering to his mysterious future until the final surrender of death itself.

Of course, even if we do achieve a new level of trust in God and freedom from our past, we will once again be tempted to make an idol of this new identity, this new God experience, and the cycle will begin all over. That is our lot as human beings. We can, however, take courage from the fact that each time we have accepted our past as past and surrendered to the future, we have met a God who could be relied on, who for all his seeming inability to protect us from the cruelties of life still was with us, still kept asking us, ''What do you want me to do for you?''

⤳ *Part Two* ⤵

Prayer and Personal Discernment

Any developing relationship between two persons will affect the whole life of each of the persons. So too, a developing relationship with God will eventually affect the whole of one's life. People who get close to God want to know God's hopes and plans for them, want to discover how best to live out the consequences of their relationship with God. In this part we take up some aspects of the search for God's will or plan.

☙ 7 ❧
God's Dream

As we saw in the first chapters, once the affective principle and foundation for the relationship with God is established a dialogue can begin between a person and God. We reveal ourselves more and more openly to God, and we can expect that God will reveal himself to us. One thing we can learn from such a dialogical prayer is God's own dream not only for each one of us but for our world. We can come to know God's dream.

In September, 1963 Martin Luther King electrified a crowd of over 200,000 people with his famous "I Have a Dream" speech. Even after the passage of 24 years his words stir the heart and bring tears to the eyes when they are read or heard on cassette or videotape.

> I have a dream that one day this nation will rise up and live out the true meaning of its creed: "We hold these truths to be self-evident, that all men are created equal."
> I have a dream that one day on the red hills of Georgia the sons of former slaves and the sons of former slave-owners will be able to sit down together at the table of brotherhood.
> I have a dream that my four little children will one day live in a nation where they will not be judged by the color of their skin but by the content of their character.

It occurred to me that many of the prophetic texts used in theAdvent liturgy express God's dream, that when we hear many of these prophecies, we hear God saying "I

have a dream. . . ." Let me spell this out a bit in this meditation.

The work of Scottish philosopher John Macmurray
has helped me to see that our belief in God the creator can
best be understood as a belief that the universe is the one
action of God, informed by one intention. To contemplate
what this means can be instructive.

We believe that this universe, with all its almost unbe-
lievable complexity, with all its eons and eons of evolution,
with its millions of years of human activity, is one action,
that it is informed, therefore, by a single intention. I find it
hard enough to imagine anyone creating a novel with all its
intricacies of plot and development of character. (The novel
is one action, and the characters do take on a life of their
own almost against the will of the author; yet the com-
pleted novel is one action of the author.)

God is creating one universe in which all of us humans
act freely, and can act contrary to God's intention. That is
what belief in a creator means. The universe is the act of
God, an act informed by one intention. This act includes
and is made up of all the actions of every human being and
all the events that will ever occur in the history of the universe. In other words, the one action of God includes the
free actions of all of us human beings, which means that the
future of God's action is not fully determinate since it depends on how we humans act. Now that is mind-
boggling—and serious—because our actions can be in tune
with God's one action or out of tune or more or less in tune,
and our happiness, even in this world, depends on how
well our actions with their intentions harmonize with
God's one action and intention.

If the universe is one action informed by one intention,
what is God's intention? We can only know with certitude
what a person intends with his action if that person reveals
his or her intention. I may, for example, try to deduce your
intention from your behavior, but my deduction would be

at best hypothetically true and at worst dead wrong. Mac-murray puts the matter tersely: "All knowledge of persons is by revelation." If this is true of human relations, how much more true of our relation with God. So the question is: Has God revealed his intention for the universe? We believe that God has done so and that we can find his intention in the Old and New Testaments. The scriptural readings for the liturgies of the Advent season provide one glimpse of God's intention.

"I have a dream," we can hear God say as we listen to these words of the prophet Isaiah.

> Many peoples will come and say,
> "Come, let us go up to the mountain of the Lord,
> to the house of the God of Jacob.
> He will teach us his ways,
> so that we may walk in his paths. . ."
> He will judge between the nations
> and will settle disputes for many peoples.
> They will beat their swords into plowshares
> and their spears into pruning hooks.
> Nation will not take up sword against nation,
> nor will they train for war anymore.
> Come, O house of Jacob,
> let us walk in the light of the Lord (Is 2:3-5).

God dreams of a universe where there will be no more wars, nor even training for war. Such a universe would be one where human beings no longer feared one another, but loved and cared for one another.

> "I have a dream," says the Lord:
> "The wolf will live with the lamb,
> the leopard will lie down with the goat,
> the calf and the lion and the yearling together;
> and a little child will lead them.
> The cow will feed with the bear,
> their young will lie down together,

and the lion will eat straw like the ox.
The infant will play near the hole of the cobra,
and the young child put his hand into the viper's
    nest.
They will neither harm nor destroy
on all my holy mountain,
for the earth will be full of the knowledge of the
    Lord
as the waters cover the sea'' (Is 11:6-9).

Let your imagination play with this revelation of God's dream. You could watch without qualms your favorite child walk into a stranger's yard where there is a pit bull terrier. You could walk anywhere in the streets of one of our large cities alone and without fear. An Irish Protestant would feel free to walk into a pub in the Catholic section of Belfast. A black American could walk at night unafraid in an all-white neighborhood. Iraqis and Iranians could have dinner together without fear of reprisals. The dread of nuclear holocaust would no longer hang like a pall over our planet.

"I have a dream," says the Lord.
"Every valley shall be raised up,
every mountain and hill made low;
the rough ground shall become level,
the rugged places a plain.
And the glory of the Lord will be revealed,
and all mankind together will see it.
For the mouth of the Lord has spoken" (Is 40:4-5).

Martin Luther King ended his string of dreams and his speech with this passage of Isaiah. Every time I hear these words, I hear Handel's setting of them in the *Messiah*, and my heart lifts with hope for our planet.

God's intention in creating the universe, it seems, is to create a place where all human beings could live as brothers and sisters in a community of faith, hope and love, united by God's Holy Spirit with Jesus Christ as sons and daughters of God, our one Father, and in harmony with the whole created universe. In his letter to the Ephesians Paul expressed his understanding of God's intention this way:

> Blessed be the God and Father of our Lord Jesus Christ. . . . For he has made known to us in all wisdom and insight the mystery of his will, according to his purpose which he set forth in Christ as a plan for the fullness of time, to unite all things in him, things in heaven and things on earth (Eph 1:3, 9-10 *RSV*).

Something deep within us is stirred by the prophetic words we have been pondering. We feel the tug of God's dream, his intention. We want to live that way, to live without the overriding fears that now bedevil all our relationships. God's own Spirit dwelling in our hearts gently, and sometimes forcefully, impels us to desire what God desires, to intend what God intends. Perhaps the surest indication that these texts do reveal God's intention for his one action which is the universe is the fact that they do stir us so deeply.

When our hearts are so stirred, we also know in our bones that we cannot exclude anyone from the reach of God's love. God's dream is for all human beings to become, in intention, what they are in fact, brothers and sisters. In his autobiographical memoir, *Sacred Journey*, Presbyterian minister Frederich Buechner recounts an event that speaks to this point. He had just signed a contract for his first novel in the offices of Alfred Knopf. As he left the office, he ran into a former college classmate who was working as a messenger boy. "I was," says Buechner, "as I thought, on the brink of fame and fortune. But instead of feeling any pride or sense of superior accomplishment by the comparison, I remember a great and unheralded rush of something like sadness, almost like shame." He reflects on

his luck and his classmate's lack of luck. Then Buechner
muses: "All I can say now is that something small but un-
forgettable happened inside me as the result of that chance
meeting—some small flickering out of the truth that, in the
long run, there can be no real joy for anybody until there is
joy finally for us all—and I can take no credit for it. . . . What
I felt was something better and truer than I was, or that I
am, and it happened, as perhaps all such things do, as a
gift." That "something better and truer" is, I believe, the
Holy Spirit of God who will not let our hearts settle for anything less than God's dream.

Almost as soon as our hearts are stirred by the dream
of God, however, another voice is heard. "It's a pipe dream
to think that we could ever attain such a state here on earth.
Maybe in heaven, but not here. This is a dog-eat-dog world
where the trusting are the losers. Even in our personal relationships we need to be careful whom we trust." Hope is
such a fragile virtue; it is so easily stifled by the voice of reason or ungodly prudence. And that voice has a powerful
motive in the fear we imbibe with our mother's milk, as it
were. We grow up fearful of the stranger, of those who are
not "one of us," of "them." But we must see the voice for
what it really is. If it stifles hope, God's dream, in us, then it
is the voice of sin, not the voice of reason. "That's the way
life is. It's naive to hope that all men and women will become brothers and sisters." This voice is not of God because it sanctions the *status quo* of mistrust and enmity between people whom God wants to be brothers and sisters
and it takes us off the hook of trying to find ways to live out
God's dream.

For that is finally the reason why God reveals his
dream to us, to stir us to act in harmony with his intention.
Unless our actions in some real way are motivated by love
and care more than fear, they, and we, are doomed to frustration. What all of us human beings want most is to live
without fear and in harmony and friendship with one an-

other. If our actions toward one another are predominantly motivated by fear, we act defensively, we are not ourselves with one another, and so we cannot become friends. If we try to distribute our actions such that those motivated by love are directed to some "in" group and those motivated by fear to "them," we will always be afraid that "they" will do something to destroy "our" community. Under these circumstances we frustrate our desires to live in peace and without fear. Moreover, some of "us" may be enticed to join "them"; so we cannot even enjoy the community we have without continued suspicion of our friends. God does not intend us to live this way; he does not intend our frustration and unhappiness. The only way we can approach happiness is by intending what God intends. The only way is to try as best we can so to act that what we do fosters the building up of the community of all human beings.

But here is the rub. We grow up in a world where fear of the other is endemic, where we learn to expect the rejection of our friendship by new people unless we earn or win their respect, where racial, ethnic, national and religious prejudice are knit into our bones. When we approach any stranger, most of us are fearful, but if that stranger is from one of the groups labeled "them" in our group, the fear can paralyze any possiblities of friendship because it is reinforced by the apperceptive mode we carry with us into the meeting; this stranger is perceived as inimical, as one of "them," before a word is exchanged. Our actions under these circumstances will tend to be motivated by fear and thus will be defensive; we will not be ourselves, nor will we be able to perceive the reality of the other. Given the pervasiveness of these fearful expectations in us, the task of attuning our actions with the one action of God seems next to possible. Here we are reminded of the cry of the apostles, "Who then can be saved?" when Jesus told them how hard it is to enter the kingdom of heaven (Mk 10:26)

And, of course, the only response we will get to our

own cry of near despair is the one Jesus gave them. "With man this is impossible, but not with God; all things are possible with God." Jesus does not water down his challenge. He does not alter reality because it seems too hard. It *is* difficult to enter the kingdom of heaven. But it is not impossible. You can, he says, attune your actions to the one action of my Father, but only by grace, by gift, by the grace of God. Rather than suppress the dream because it seems impossible of attainment, we must allow it to take deep root in our hearts, to convince us of its attractiveness, to elicit our own desires for its attainment and, then, like the blind beggar Bartimaeus, beg that whatever in us hinders us from trying to attain the dream be healed. The greatest hindrance is our fear and all the self-other schemata or expectations we have built up to protect ourselves from what we fear. We must beg God to heal our fears, to give us hopeful expectations, to help us to act out of love rather than fear. "All things are possible with God."

"I have a dream," God says whenever we pay close attention to the prophets of the Old Testament. He wants us to share that dream. And our happiness, even in this earthly life, lies in such sharing, and in acting in tune with that dream. Let us allow God's dream to stir our hearts to desire its fulfillment even in our days.

⊂⋘ 8 ⋙⊃

But Can We Live Out God's Dream?

We all know that one person's good news is often another's bad news. The farmer prays for rain and is overjoyed when it comes, but the vacationer is miserable. In athletic contests the victors' smiles are balanced by the losers' tears. Both sides in a war pray for victory, but at most only one can be satisfied. It makes a thoughtful person wonder about some prayers of petition. Our purpose here, however, is not to deal with that difficult question, but rather to have us look at instances when what, to all appearances, should be good news is experienced as bad. The issue already rose in the last chapter when we echoed the distressed question of the apostles, "Who then can be saved?" Here I am thinking quite particularly of a close reading of the text of the First Letter of John, chapter 4, verses 7 to 21. At first blush it sounds like good news indeed; but a closer reading can and does turn it into bad news for many people. I want to make sure that we see the deep hole the text can dig for us, and then I want to propose a way out.

> Dear friends, let us love one another, for love comes from God. Everyone who loves has been born of God and knows God. Whoever does not love does not know God, because God is love. This is how God showed his love among us: He sent his one and only son into the world that we might live through him. This is love: not that we loved God, but that he loved us and sent his Son as an atoning sacrifice for

our sins. Dear friends, since God so loved us, we
also ought to love each other. No one has ever seen
God; but if we love one another, God lives in us and
his love is made complete in us.

We know that we live in him and he in us, because he has given us of his Spirit. And we have
seen and testify that the Father has sent his Son to
be the Savior of the world. If anyone acknowledges
that Jesus is the Son of God, God lives in him and he
in God. And so we know and rely on the love God
has for us.

God is love. Whoever lives in love lives in God,
and God in him. In this way love is made complete
among us so that we will have confidence on the
day of judgment, because in this world we are like
him. There is no fear in love. But perfect love drives
out fear, because fear has to do with punishment.
The one who fears is not made perfect in love.

We love because he first loved us. If anyone says,
"I love God," yet hates his brother, he is a liar. For
anyone who does not love his brother, whom he has
seen, cannot love God, whom he has not seen. And
he has given us this command: Whoever loves God
must also love his brother.

First, the good news. Twice the text affirms: "God is
love." Moreover, the author asserts: "This is how God
showed his love among us: He sent his one and only Son
into the world that we might live through him. This is love:
not that we loved God, but that he loved us and sent his
Son as an atoning sacrifice for our sins." Good news indeed! The author seems to have distilled the essence of the
teaching of Jesus: God, total Mystery, Creator and Ruler of
the universe, the awesome One, is "Abba," "dear
Daddy," "dear Mommy." To let such a revelation of the
very nature of God sink home brings an incredible freedom, lightness and joy, a further deepening of the affective
first principle and foundation.

A closer look at the text, however, can disperse the joy. "Everyone who loves has been born of God and knows God. Whoever does not love does not know God, because God is love." "Dear friends, since God so loved us, we also ought to love one another. No one has ever seen God; but if we love one another, God lives in us and his love is made complete in us." Who can pass this litmus test? It reminds us of those impossible words of Jesus: "Be perfect, therefore, as your heavenly Father is perfect" (Mt 5:48). Who can love as God loves? If we do not so love, then, according to the text, we have no guarantee that God dwells in us or that we know God at all. An honest look at our hearts will reveal a barrel full of prejudices, envies, dislikes, resentments, and even hatreds. The good news has turned bad in a hurry.

Further we read: "God is love. Whoever lives in love lives in God, and God in him. In this way, love is made complete among us so that we will have confidence on the day of judgment, because in this world we are like him." What confidence could the author mean? Are we really like God in the way we love, forgive, live our daily lives? And the author drives home the point, it seems, a little further on. "If anyone says, 'I love God,' yet hates his brother, he is a liar. For anyone who does not love his brother, whom he has seen, cannot love God, whom he has not seen. And he has given us this command: Whoever loves God must also love his brother." We will approach the judgment seat of God in fear and trembling rather than with confidence if these are the standards by which we will be judged.

The text also says: "There is no fear in love. But perfect love drives out fear, because fear has to do with punishment. The one who fears is not made perfect in love." We know ourselves as shot through with fears. We are afraid of what the neighbors will think of us. We are afraid that our houses will be broken into or that we will be mugged in the streets. We are afraid that we will lose our jobs or our savings. We are afraid of people who are different from ourselves; whites and blacks are afraid of each other as are communists and capitalists, Jews and Arabs, Protestants and Catholics, rich and poor. We are afraid of ourselves, and we are afraid of death. Obviously we have not been made perfect in love.

Perhaps it does not pay to give scripture texts too close a look. Very quickly good news turns bad when one does so. The more closely we read this text, which seems to have been written for our consolation, the less confidence we have against the day of judgment. Moreover, we know that good resolutions to love others and to cast out fear do about as much good as our new year's resolutions. They are honored as much or more in the breach as in the observance. In addition, the failure of our resolutions to be more loving can bring us to doubt the possibility of ever being a Christian in deed. Despair lurks around the corner.

Perhaps we can find a way out of our dilemma by giving some thought to the way we are changed by any friendship or love relationship. We are first attracted by another person. We like John's looks, for example, and we want to know him better. Or we admire the way Joan treats other people with respect and seems to put all her attention on the person she's with. Most especially we like the way she treats us. So we try to spend time with the person who attracts us. We want to get to know the person better. As mutuality develops, what happens? The two people begin to share more and more of themselves with one another. Each gets to know the other's attitudes, hopes, dreams, desires, values. Each also begins, almost imperceptibly, to take on the admired characteristics of the other. It is not as though they make resolutions to be like the other; in fact, if they try that route, they find themselves failing and become discouraged, even doubtful about being worthy of the other's friendship. No; gradually, almost by osmosis, we begin to react to and value and look at the world as the other does.

We even come to like the people the other likes when at first we could not understand what our friend saw in these people. When two people have spent years together, they often vote the same way, like the same books and movies and people, share the same kinds of prayer and worship, talk the same way and even finish one another's sentences. Some old married couples even begin to look alike, they say.

These reflections on friendship and love bring us close to a way out of our dilemma. In the gospels we are told a few times that Jesus went off by himself to pray. One gets the impression that this was a practice with him. In this communing with God he came to know God intimately as "Abba." Could it not be that this communing, this development of an intimate relationship with God, was the way that the human Jesus grew like God? In other words, Jesus spent time with God in intimate conversation, in prayer, and in the process became more and more imbued with the values and attitudes of God. He took on the mind and heart of God. Thus, he could love as God loves, forgive as God forgives, heal as God heals, feel compassion as God does. Perhaps we can understand in this way the statement: "And Jesus grew in wisdom and stature, and in favor with God and men" (Lk 2:52). No wonder the same writer can report these words at Jesus' baptism: "And a voice came from heaven: 'You are my Son, whom I love; with you I am well pleased' " (Lk 3:22).

If Jesus became an imitator of God through prayer, we can follow his example. The very fact that we are reading this book indicates our attraction to God and the things of God. We do desire "I know not what," the Mystery we call God. We need to trust that desire in us and trust that in God there is a reciprocal desire for intimacy with us as individuals as well as with us as a community. If we do put our trust in this reciprocity of desires, then we will want to spend time getting to know God better. We will, in other

words, take time for prayer that gives God a chance to reveal his heart to us and gives us a chance to open our hearts
to God. Gradually, like Jesus, we will become more like
God in our attitudes, our values, our loves and hates. But it
will be by osmosis, not resolution; by grace, not by dint of
our heroic efforts.

Scripture is, of course, the privileged place to find out
about God. We can read parts of the Bible with the desire
that God use the words and stories there to reveal himself
to us. There are many sources that can help us to use scripture in this way to develop our relationship with God, some
of which I mention in the bibliography at the end of this
book.

If we would be imitators of God, we can do nothing
more helpful than to get to know Jesus better. He is *the* human image of God *par excellence*. In Jesus we find enfleshed
the mind and heart of God. If we would be perfect as our
heavenly Father is perfect, then we can do no better than to
develop an intimate relationship with Jesus. Here again the
gospels are the privileged place for meeting him. We can
read the gospels with the desire of Ignatius of Loyola: that I
may know Jesus more intimately in order that I may love
him more and follow him more closely. Notice that this desire asks for a grace, a revelation of Jesus to me. I can read
the gospels over and over, but I will not come to know Jesus
intimately if he does not touch my heart in some way, if he
does not reveal himself to me. Once again, however, we
can count on a reciprocal desire in Jesus to reveal himself. In
the very place where he enjoins on his followers the command to love one another, he also calls them friends.

> "My command is this: Love each other as I have
> loved you. Greater love has no one than this, that
> one lay down his life for his friends. You are my
> friends if you do what I command. I no longer call
> you servants, because a servant does not know his

master's business. Instead, I have called you friends, for everything that I learned from my Father I have made known to you. You did not choose me, but I chose you and appointed you to go and bear fruit—fruit that will last. Then the Father will give you whatever you ask in my name. This is my command: Love each other" (Jn 15:12-17).

The key to understanding this passage as well as the passage in the First Letter of John as good news lies in the wonder that Jesus offers us friendship, a friendship that we can allow to develop and deepen by spending time with him. If we do so, we will gradually grow more like him. Just as the disciples were not made perfect in love by their three years of close friendship with him, so too it will take time with us. If God and Jesus, God's Son, are willing to work patiently with us to develop the relationship, then we can have patience with ourselves. We do not need to be heroes of ascetical practice, giants of the will, in order to be made perfect in love. All we need to do is to take time to get to know God, Father, Son, and Holy Spirit, better. All we need is to keep alive the desire for God and the desire to know Jesus more intimately, and God will do the rest.

"I am the vine; you are the branches. If a man remains in me and I in him, he will bear much fruit; apart from me you can do nothing. . . . If you remain in me and my words remain in you, ask whatever you wish, and it will be given you. This is to my Father's glory, that you bear much fruit, showing yourselves to be my disciples" (Jn 15: 5-8). Good news indeed!

⚜ 9 ⚜

What Is God Really Like?

In a letter to the editor of *The Church World*, Maine's Catholic weekly (March 10, 1988), a woman wrote: "Genuine love is not permissive. . . . With the excuse that God is love, we permit ourselves every wrong. Don't let us make of Him a *weakling*." Behind these pithy and strong words one senses an anger that all this talk of God's love has not led us to live more Christian and moral lives, nor has it made the world a better place to bring up children. Maybe, she seems to indicate, we need to hear more about God's wrath.

Her letter, I believe, raises an even larger issue that troubles many of us and has a disturbing influence on our relationship with God. It is all well and good to affirm that God is love, but is it really unconditional love, as many today proclaim? Many of the Old Testament readings at Sunday Mass do not seem to bear out a theory of unconditional love, for example this text from the Second Book of Chronicles.

> The Lord, the God of their fathers, sent word to them through his messengers again and again, because he had pity on his people and on his dwelling place. But they mocked God's messengers, despised his words and scoffed at his prophets until the wrath of the Lord was aroused against his people and there was no remedy (2 Chr 36:15-16).

It seems that God's love has its limits, that it is conditional on our shaping up. Worse yet, God seems to change into a vengeful God. "He [God] brought up against them the king of the Babylonians, who killed their young men with the sword in the sanctuary, and spared neither young man nor young woman, old man or aged. God handed all of them over to Nebuchadnezzar'' (2 Chr 36:17).

Lest we think that these images of a wrathful God have been superseded by the proclamation of Jesus in the New Testament, we need only remind ourselves of the judgment scene depicted by Jesus in Matthew 25, ''Depart from me, you who are cursed, into the eternal fire prepared for the devil and his angels. For I was hungry and you gave me nothing to eat. . .'' (Mt 25: 41 ff.). All of us tremble in our depths when we hear these words of Jesus. Will we face a God of love or a God of wrath when we face our Maker?

Moreover, since each of us knows in our hearts that we continually fall short of our own best aspirations, let alone of the high standards to which Jesus called us, our prayer life may well be affected. How can we expect to have a close relationship with God, Father, Son, and Spirit, when we feel ourselves so deeply unworthy and worse still a possible target of God's wrath? We do not easily move close to someone from whom we expect a bawling out or worse.

However, on the same fourth Sunday of Lent when this text is read, we also hear the following words from John's gospel:

> ''For God so loved the world that he gave his one and only Son, that whoever believes in him shall not perish but have eternal life. For God did not send his Son into the world to condemn the world, but to save the world through him. Whoever believes in him is not condemned, but whoever does not believe stands condemned already because he has not believed in the name of God's one and only Son'' (Jn 3:16-18).

This text prompts a meditation that may show us a way out of our dilemma and help us to overcome our fears of condemnation. It may also help us to see that a God of love is not a weakling.

The text suggests to me that we distinguish between God and our experience of God. It will be my contention that God remains the same even when we experience him differently. It sounds like a truism, but the distinction is very difficult to make in practice.

What do we believe about God? We believe that God is the perfect community. The three persons are so united with one another that they share everything in common; the only difference between them is their mutual relationships to one another. When we human beings love someone very much, one of our pains is that we cannot be completely one with the beloved. It may be that this experience of pain derives from the fact that we are pale images of the triune God. In God the three Persons are so one that the only distinguishing marks are their relationships to one another. Hence, in the community that is God there can be no disunity, no separation, no fear. God is the perfect community of which even the best human relationship or the best human community we can imagine is only a pale carbon. Hence, God, even apart from his creation, is not lonely and in need of companionship. If he creates, it is not out of need, but out of superabounding generosity and love, as if the three Persons were to say: "This community of ours is so good; let's share the goodness."

As we noted earlier, Sebastian Moore asserts (in *Let This Mind Be in You*) that God's desire for a universe makes that universe to be, and to be desirable, just as God's desire for each one of us makes each one of us to be, and to be desirable. Moreover, we have already theorized that God created the universe with one intention, that it be a place where each spiritual being (including us humans) would share God's community life of mutual love and affection. "And he made known to us the mystery of his will according to his good pleasure, which he purposed in Christ, to be put into effect when the times will have reached their fulfillment—to bring all things in heaven and on earth together under one head, even Christ'' (Eph 1: 9-10). I believe that we can read the words of John 3 cited earlier to mean that God has not changed his mind from the beginning of creation; he intends a community of love because he is love. So he always faces the universe and each one of us with love, not condemnation.

Now, how do we experience God? Every so often, as we said earlier, we experience a sense of joy and desire for ''we know not what'' that lets us know that we are the apple of God's eye, that we are at home in the universe, that we are safe and saved. This experience warms us and at the same time lets us know that our hearts are restless until they rest in ''we know not what,'' the Mystery we call God. Experiences like these are the affective first principle and foundation, the ''Abba'' experience Jesus pointed to, the experience of being held in the warm embrace of God, our Abba (Father), that enables us to trust ourselves and our world as a homely place. We also have experiences of knowing in our hearts that our sins have been forgiven by God. We have looked at the crucifix, for example, and felt there that those wonderful words of Jesus, ''Father, forgive them for they do not know what they are doing,'' were also spoken on our behalf. So we do have experiences that tell us that God is love indeed.

But we also have other experiences that leave us quaking. In the presence of a God of so much goodness and love we feel ashamed, guilt-ridden, unworthy. We wonder whether we will see compassion and forgiveness in the eyes of Jesus when we realize how often we fail to live up to his standards. We focus on the blazing anger Jesus showed toward the Pharisees, those ''whitened sepulchres,'' and fear to look him in the eye. We expect to hear those terrible words Jesus directed at Peter, ''Get behind me, Satan'' (Mk 8: 33). In other words, we recoil from God and from Jesus, expecting their wrath and punishment, and we interpret our experience as a reaction to God's or Jesus' changed attitude toward us. But have they changed? Or have we changed? We need to look at this experience of recoil to discern what is of God in it and what is of our own making.

The first question we have to ask ourselves is: What is our fundamental attitude toward God, Jesus and life in general? Are we believers or unbelievers? Are we people who in spite of our frailty and sinfulness want to live good, Christian lives or not? In workshops on discernment I often have people read the first two rules for discernment formulated by St. Ignatius in his *Spiritual Exercises*. In condensed form here they are:

> 1. In the case of those who go from one mortal sin to another, the enemy is ordinarily accustomed to propose apparent pleasures. He fills their imagination with sensual delights and gratifications. . . . With such persons the good spirit uses a method which is the reverse. . . . he will rouse the sting of conscience and fill them with remorse.
>
> 2. In the case of those who go on earnestly striving to cleanse their souls from sin,. . . the method pursued is the opposite. . . . Then it is characteristic of the evil spirit to harass with anxiety, to afflict with sadness, to raise obstacles backed by fallacious reasonings that disturb. . . . It is characteristic of the good spirit, however, to give courage and strength, consolations, tears, inspirations, and peace.

I then ask the audience to reflect on their own lives to see into which category they best fit. Those who attend such workshops are obviously not on the road to perdition. Nor, I would venture to say, are those who read and take seriously books such as this.

What does such a reflection signify in discerning the meaning of the recoil reactions we mentioned earlier? If they trouble our hearts and keep us from praying trustingly to God, they cannot be of God's Spirit. After all, if God wants us to reform our lives in some way, he will move us to seek his help, his forgiveness, his grace, not to run away from him. When the prodigal son finally came to his senses, he was moved to run back to his father, not to run further away in fear. If our fears of God's anger lead us away from prayer, away from trust in the goodness and kindness of God, then we are obviously not experiencing God since God wants us to come closer, to trust his mercy and love. In this case, in other words, we are projecting wrath and anger onto God. God has not changed; we have changed our image of him.

If there ever was a moment when God might have washed his hands of us in wrath, that moment occurred when we human beings crucified his one and only Son, Jesus. In Jesus God had done all that he could to call us into his community life, and we, as it were, threw it back in his face. We killed the loveliest gift God ever gave, and killed him shamefully, in an ugly fashion. Yet at the very moment when our fate, it seemed, hung in the balance, Jesus, the human heart of God, asked forgiveness for us. He still looked on us with love, thus proving beyond a doubt that God really is love. Perhaps what breaks God's heart most is our extreme difficulty in believing what every crucifix in the world proclaims.

At this point someone might object: "But doesn't God have standards? God's love cannot be totally permissive." Surely God has standards. God wants what is for our best interests. He wants us to live as brothers and sisters of Jesus Christ and in harmony with the whole created universe. His Spirit dwelling in our hearts continually moves us to live out our lives in tune with God's intention for the universe. When we are out of tune, the malaise we feel indicates that we are not right with God and with our best selves. But when we are out of tune, God does not change toward us; rather we have, in some minor or major fashion, changed our direction toward God.

Well, what about the existence of hell? Doesn't that prove that God's love is conditioned on our performance? Here again, we would have to say that it is possible for someone to refuse God's friendship absolutely. God not only will not, but he cannot coerce our friendship, our acceptance of who he is. Hell, whatever it is, is not of God's making. Indeed, it may be his ultimate heartbreak that he could not convince someone to trust him.

Is God a weakling? Is it weakness to love someone enough to die for that person? Is it weakness to refuse to destroy someone who mocks and derides you? Is it weakness to continue to hold out the hand of friendship no matter how outrageous the other treats you? If for us the cross makes God out to be a weakling, then we are of all people foolish indeed.

⚛ 10 ⚛

The Kingdom of God and Discernment

Once Daniel Harrington, S.J., New Testament professor at Weston School of Theology, editor of *New Testament Abstracts*, and friend, deftly and kindly corrected a phrase that had become a cliche with me. I had used the phrase "building up the kingdom" almost as a throwaway line at the end of a piece I had written. "Nothing in scripture," Dan said, "justifies talk about the building up of the kingdom of God." I decided that I had better clean up my act in this regard, or it would recur. In the course of studying the biblical meaning of the phrase, "the kingdom of God," I had an idea that may be a spur to our discernment of how to live in tune with God.

New Testament scholars are agreed that the centerpiece of Jesus' preaching was the kingdom or reign of God, but it is not so easy to know what Jesus understood by the phrase. Kenneth Leech (*Experiencing God: Theology As Spirituality*) believes that the facts can best be understood by a series of negations. "Firstly, the Kingdom of God in the New Testament is not an otherworldly hope," a heaven peopled by the souls of the saved. When Jesus says, "My Kingdom is not of this world," he does not mean that it is or will be located someplace else, but that its origins and values are from God, are immanent only as transcendent. Indeed, when they become immanent, they are met with opposition and struggle precisely because they are "not of this world."

"Secondly, the Kingdom of God is not seen as a grad-

77

ual, evolutionary movement." Suddenness and surprise are more the flavor of Jesus' parables of the kingdom. One gets the sense that people will be shocked when they find out what God's reign means and who actually accepts that reign much as Mrs. Turpin in Flannery O'Connor's short story *Revelation* is shocked by her vision of a vast swinging bridge.

> Upon it a vast horde of souls were rumbling toward heaven. There were whole companies of white-trash, clean for the first time in their lives, and bands of black niggers in white robes, and battalions of freaks and lunatics shouting and clapping and leaping like frogs. And bringing up the end of the procession was a tribe of people whom she recognized at once as those who, like herself and Claud, had always had a little of everything and the God-given wit to use it right. . . . They were marching behind the others with great dignity, accountable as they had always been for good order and common sense and respectable behavior. They alone were on key. Yet she could see by their shocked and altered faces that even their virtues were being burned away.

"Thirdly, the Kingdom of God is not an individual, inner experience," is not, in other words, a Leibnitzian "preestablished harmony" of monads. It is, of course, an inner experience, but an experience that depends on community and tends toward the forming of community.

"Fourthly, the Kingdom of God is not wholly future." It is both present and future. In Jesus' preaching the Kingdom of God is both now—and not yet.

"Finally, it must be emphasized that the Kingdom of God is not the same as the Church." In fact, it was my too facile identification of the two that led to my speaking of the building up of the kingdom. The church is the proclaimer of the kingdom and a sacrament of the kingdom, but not the kingdom itself. Nor is membership in the church as such a guarantee of being finally under the reign of God.

Put positively, then, the kingdom or reign of God is immanent in this universe, yet transcendent, is present and is not yet present, is and will be experienced as a surprising, disturbing presence, is immanent and not yet immanent in individuals, but only as part of a community, and is only presaged by the church while yet being immanent in the church. In truth, the kingdom of God seems to bear all the characteristics of God, the Creator and Lord of the universe who is both transcendent to and immanent in the universe and who is experienced by individuals only insofar as they are part of a community.

Given this understanding of the kingdom of God it is obvious that we do not build up or even help to build up the Kingdom. God alone effects his reign; or to put it even more strongly, God alone is God, i.e., is the reign of God. The question is: Do we have any role to play?

Although the kingdom of God is equated with God, there would be no need of such a concept if there were no created universe. We can understand the kingdom of God as God's intention for the universe, or rather as God's one action which is the universe, to use again the words of John Macmurray. According to Macmurray any action of a person is guided by an intention. For example, I intended to write this book. That intention makes the writing of the book with all that went into it one action. I am immanent in this one action, but I am also transcendent to it. I express myself, but I am not the book. So too, Macmurray argues, one can only think the universe as God's one action informed by one intention. Just as we humans are immanent in, yet transcendent to our actions, so too, and *a fortiori*, is God. God's one action includes all of the events (non-personal) and all the actions (personal) that constitute the history of the universe.

Just as we cannot know the intention of any person's

action except by the revelation of that person, all the more
we cannot know God's one intention except by his revelation. Even then we will only know darkly and by faith. We
have already argued that God has revealed his intention for
our world, namely that all human beings live as brothers
and sisters in a community of faith, hope and love united
with Jesus Christ as sons and daughters of God, our Father
and in harmony with the whole created universe.

   This notion of one action seems to coincide with the
characteristics of the kingdom of God enumerated earlier.
It is immanent, yet transcendent; it is this-wordly, yet is an
action of God; it is a surprising, even shocking presence because it includes the whole world and demands the break-
down of all sectarian and national divisions; it is only experienced in community, and, in fact, is not yet realized as
long as any individual or group is in principle excluded
from the community; it is quite obviously not simply
equated with the church, even if the church is conceived as
the union of all Christian churches since God's one action
includes the whole world and all its people.

   But the question of our role in this one action of God
must still be addresssed. If we do not build up the kingdom
of God, i.e., if we do not build up or create the one action
God intends, what do we do or can we do? Again Macmurray affords a clue to the answer. If the universe is one action
of God, then our own actions can be in tune with this one
action or not. Insofar as our actions are in tune, we are satisfied and fulfilled; insofar as they are not, we are and will be
frustrated in our intentions. In other words, God's one intention will be achieved because God is God. We can be
more or less satisfied in life depending on whether we are
in tune with God's one action. And insofar as we are in
tune, the kingdom of God is immanent in us. To the extent
that we are in tune with God's one action, to that extent our
actions, by God's grace, intend the community of all people
and try to let that community emerge. We try, with God's

grace, in the concrete circumstances of our lives to cooperate with others to overcome fears and hatreds, to create a climate and institutions where humans are enabled to live together as brothers and sisters.

That is our role. To be fulfilled and really happy in this life we need to let our hearts become attuned to the one action of God, to let God's intention for our world guide our actions. Prayer, disciplined reflection and discernment, then, are urgently needed, not in order to build up the kingdom, but to know where it is and to be truly happy. Traditional language speaks of the discernment of God's will. If we take the will of God as the intention which informs his one action which is the kingdom of God, we may, perhaps, be able to broaden our understanding of what discernment means.

First of all, Christians who have not yet made a permanent commitment to a way of life in the church (e.g., the vocations of marriage, religious life, priesthood, lay ministry, missionary, etc.) have the opportunity to discern which way of life is more in tune for each of them with God's one action, given their temperament, talent, upbringing, societal constraints and previous choices in life. The question for discernment would come down to which way of life is more fulfilling, challenging and satisfying for me since the more I am in tune with God's one action, the more deeply satisfied I will be.

Secondly, no matter what way of life I have chosen—and, indeed, no matter whether it was a well-discerned choice or not—I am presented each day with a myriad of choices about how to live my life, some of them trivial, others more substantial, even momentous. "What dress shall I wear?" "Should I ask my boss for a raise?" "Shall I tell the children about my diagnosis of cancer?" "Shall we have meat loaf for dinner?" "Should I say something to John about his drinking?" "Should I talk to Helen about how angry she made me last night?" "Shall I accept the new job

I've been offered?'' ''How shall I vote in today's election?''
These and many other choices confront us daily. Once
again in responding to the more substantial ones we can be
more or less in tune with the one action of God.

In order to become discerning, we need practice in
prayerful attention to the movements of our hearts, prayerful reflection on them, and honest appraisal of what seems
more in tune with God's one action. What leads to greater
faith, hope and love in our hearts? What seems more likely
to enhance real communion and community among those
with whom we live and work? Conversely, which alterna-
tive seems to close us more in on ourselves and make us
more fearful and self-protective? A daily examination of
consciousness would gradually make us more fine-tuned
as to what choices are more in line with God's kingdom.
We would become more discerning of where the kingdom
is present.

Finally, we live in a world of social, political, economic, cultural and religious institutions that are human
creations and that condition our lives and our choices. Lux-
uries of 20 years ago are necessities today, for example. ''I
need my word processor to do my apostolate.'' ''I couldn't
live in a place without running hot water.'' ''We have to
watch the evening news on T.V.'' ''No one can get along
without a car.''

Moreover, cultural stereotypes condition how we react to people of a different race or ethnic origin. To take another example, 30 years ago a Roman Catholic culture dom-
inated the lives of most Catholics to such an extent that they
never seriously questioned that eating meat on Friday was
so serious an offense that one merited eternal damnation
for deliberately doing so. These examples illustrate how we
are conditioned by social and cultural institutions and customs which are human creations.

But as human creations these institutions and customs
are not automatically in tune with God's one action which

is his kingdom. As Christians we are called to discern in this area as well as in our personal and interpersonal lives. What structures in our church and our churches, for example, militate against God's intention of a universal community of brothers and sisters in the Lord? A clear example would be racial or ethnic exclusivity. Segregated churches are obviously not where the kingdom of God is present. But we might ask whether the structures which systematically exclude women from the ministry of the word and altar (e.g., the prohibition against women deacons and priests and even against altar girls) are in tune with the intention of God?

In the social and political realm we must discern whether the institutions human beings have created are in tune with God's one action. The bishops of the United States, for example, have asked precisely that question with regard to the nuclear arms policy and the economic structures and policies of the United States. Christians need to ask such questions about the health care system of their country and about its foreign policy among other things. At the local level the basic ecclesial communities of South America ask such questions about the social, economic and political structures and policies that impinge on people's lives and make it more or less possible to live as brothers and sisters in the Lord.

In these and many other instances discernment is very difficult and fraught with potential for conflict. It will require much prayer, reading, reflection and dialogue among the people of God and among all people of good will. We do have instances in which the process has worked and institutions more amenable to the values of the kingdom have been created. Moreover, the process undertaken by the bishops of the United States in developing their pastorals on peace and on the economy provide a model for such discernment.

Jesus was the human being most perfectly in tune with

the one action of God, and so in him preeminently and uniquely the kingdom of God was present and is present. But the ''not yet'' was also in evidence because he could not persuade even his closest followers that being in tune with the one action of God was for their good no matter what the consequences. Their fears and prejudices got in the way. Earlier we noted with Leech that the kingdom of God is not an evolving movement. Since we cannot honestly say or even opine that in our age a higher percentage of people are in tune with God's one action than in Jesus' age, that truth is hardly in jeopardy. Even the holiest among us, and per- haps they most of all, are aware of how far they are from being wholly in tune with God's one action. A short exami- nation of conscience and a look at the newspapers or at the evening news will let any of us know how far we are as indi- viduals and communities from being in tune with God's one action. The extent to which we fall short is so stagger- ing as to plunge us into depair. Indeed, I wonder if the ''bread and circuses'' of our time, e.g., the inanity of much of our entertainment, the conspicious consumption of lux- ury items, the abuse of alcohol, drugs and sex, are not ways of staving off the honest look that might lead to despair.

But Jesus looked reality in the eye if any human ever did, and he did not despair. He must have caught glimpses of the kingdom of God, of the power of love to overcome fear and hatred, and he put his faith in that power. He knew that the powers of darkness would try to quench the light, but they would not prevail. They might seem to pre- vail, but God's light (his action) would not be quenched.

Jesus was assailed by all the powers of evil. Like any human being he feared suffering and death. He wanted his Jewish brothers and sisters to believe in and trust Yahweh as Abba and so he did not relish their rejection. He wanted Judas as a friend and companion and must have recoiled at the kiss of betrayal. But he trusted in Abba to see him through, and so these evils were nothing ultimately to be afraid of. We, too, can beg Jesus to help us to trust in God and to show us how to grow more and more attuned to the kingdom of God, more discerning of the presence of that kingdom in our world. At the same time may he help us to recognize that every such discernment is still only a glimpse, a foretaste of that reign which is the culmination of God's intention, "to unite all things in him."

Part Three

Some Issues of Communal Discernment

The previous chapter introduced the notion of the effect of social structures on our attempts to live out God's dream for our world. Not only do we need to be discerning as individuals in regard to such structures, but we also need to act in concert with others to change those structures that are inimical to God's intention. To do so we must be able to discern communally, to pray and reflect together to find God's will. In the three following chapters we shall look at some ways of doing such communal discernment that may have practical consequences for how we shall be church.

ᄋᄌ 11 ᄋᄃ

The Battle With Demons

Each of the three synoptic gospels has an account of Christ's temptation in the desert. In contrast to the accounts of the temptation provided by Matthew and Luke, Mark's could have been written by your proverbial Vermont Yankee who wastes no words. "At once the Spirit sent him out into the desert, and he was in the desert forty days, being tempted by Satan. He was with the wild animals, and angels attended him" (Mk 1:12-13). Mark seems almost impatient to get to the story of Jesus' public life, unwilling to be bothered with the details of the struggle in the desert. These brief words, however, contain a motif that runs like a thread throughout Mark's narrative: Jesus' presence is a direct attack on the "evil empire" of Satan.

The very first healing, which comes immediately after the call of the first disciples, is the cure of a man possessed by an evil spirit. The demon knew Jesus and "cried out, 'What do you want with us, Jesus of Nazareth? Have you come to destroy us? I know who you are—the Holy One of God.' 'Be quiet!' said Jesus sternly. 'Come out of him!' The evil spirit shook the man violently and came out of him with a shriek" (Mk 1:24-26). This pattern of conflict—the evil spirits recognize who Jesus is, Jesus commands their silence and their departure, they leave violently—occurs a number of times in the gospel. The combat is mortal indeed, and nowhere is this so apparent as in chapter 5 where Jesus, by a simple word, expels the legion of demons who have tormented one man and made him so violently strong that "no one could bind him any more, not even with a

chain. For he had often been chained hand and foot, but he
tore the chains apart and broke the irons on his feet. No one
was strong enough to subdue him. Night and day among
the tombs and in the hills he would cry out and cut himself
with stones" (Mk 5:3-5). In Mark's gospel the casting out of
demons is a central aspect of Jesus' ministry.

In addition, in chapter 3 we read: "Jesus went up into
the hills and called to him those he wanted, and they came
to him. He appointed twelve—designating them apostles—
that they might be with him and that he might send them
out to preach and to have authority to drive out demons"
(Mk 3:13-15). Jesus gives the apostles the same ministry he
has, preaching the good news and casting out demons. Finally, in the section after the resurrection which is not in the
most reliable early manuscripts the thread is continued:
"He said to them, 'Go into all the world and preach the
good news to all creation. Whoever believes and is baptized
will be saved, but whoever does not believe will be con-
demned. And these signs will accompany those who believe: In my name they will drive out demons. . .' " (Mk 16:
15-17). Apparently, the battle with demons is expected to
continue throughout the history of the church.

Usually when we meditate on these scenes of mortal
combat between Jesus and the "evil one," we think in intrapersonal terms. We ponder our own inner demons, our
tendencies toward sinful jealousy, resentment, lust, despair, addiction, etc. Sometimes we might even think in interpersonal terms and consider the demons that beset our
closest relationships; for example, the lack of mutual understanding, toleration and trust that often makes family
life so painfully difficult. These intrapersonal and interpersonal tendencies can seem so intractable and poisonous as
to be attributable to the presence of the "evil one." Depression, for example, can make a person feel so desolate, lost
and desperate that both the person and those who try to
help feel as helpless as the man with the legion of demons

and those who tried to bind him. Relations between family members can become so embittered and tangled that reconciliation seems like a pipe dream. Faced by such seemingly intractable situations we may, like the disciples, be tempted to despair. They asked Jesus one time, "Why couldn't we drive it [the demon] out?" When we are tempted to despair, we can remember Jesus' reply: "This kind can come out only by prayer" (Mk 9: 28-29). Of course, we need to use every other means toward effecting a solution as well. But, finally, we need to entrust ourselves and those in need to the saving power of God.

Rather than concentrate on intra- and interpersonal demons, however, I want to suggest a reflection on another realm where our "demons" are even more insidious, hidden and intractable. We humans live not only in an intra- and interpersonal world but also in a world of social, political, cultural and religious institutions, structures and ambience that condition everything we experience and do. For want of a better term I will call this realm the social-cultural dimension of human existence. A few examples will illustrate what is meant by the term.

Recently I visited Ireland on my way to Rome. Every time I started to cross a street, I first looked left and tended to start across if I saw no traffic; only then would I look right to check for traffic coming the other way. Needless to say, there were a few close calls since the nearer oncoming traffic came from my right. In the United States my habitual mode of checking for traffic before crossing a street is not only second nature, but also self-protective. In Ireland it was still second nature, but downright dangerous since traffic runs in what I took as the "wrong" direction. Here is a simple example of a social institution, the patterning of traffic, that conditioned my behavior without my being aware of the conditioning.

I go to the store to buy toothpaste, and my first inclination is to pick up Brand X. If someone were to ask me why I

chose X, I might volunteer that it's better for fighting cavi-
ties. In fact, I have no guarantee that I am correct, but I have
been conditioned to behave in this fashion by advertise-
ments on T.V. and in newspapers and magazines. Name
recognition may well be the real motivation for the choice.
A social institution (modern advertising) has conditioned
my behavior.

More seriously, let's imagine ourselves walking down
a street in an unfamiliar neighborhood. I see a group of
teenagers approaching me. They are not of my racial background. I notice myself getting tense and nervous and begin to think of an unobtrusive way of crossing the street.
Five minutes earlier I had passed a group of teenagers of my
own racial background without a quaver. Again, we see
how behavior is conditioned by cultural stereotypes.

Jesuit social activist William Callahan believes that we
are all cultural addicts. Men in the United States, for example, are socialized into being competitive with one another
and into fearing that any signs of affection for another man
are homosexual. On the broader scale educated, middle-
class Americans share many unarticulated cultural values
and expectations. Body odors are anathema, for example.
Running hot water, three square meals a day, with snacks
in between, a relatively full refrigerator and larder, T.V.
and a car at one's disposal or at least available for use
through negotiation, money for movies and other entertainment, these are only a few of the expectations middle-
class Americans share. We expect that hard work will be rewarded and tend to assume that lack of such rewards
results from laziness. We accept what social scientists call
the "just world hypothesis" and thus tend to presume that
the victims of calamities such as rape, a mutilating accident
or endemic poverty are somehow responsible for their
plight. Callahan makes the point of our cultural addiction
with a trenchant example: "It is far more difficult for an
American to relate to a loving, honest, virtuous person who

is dirty or smelly, than to relate to a dishonest, unscrupulous, exploitive person who is neat and well-mannered" (*Soundings*). All of us have subconscious racial and ethnic stereotypes that we imbibe with mother's milk, as it were, and which condition many of our reactions to other people. Blacks and whites in the U. S.,Protestants and Catholics in Northern Ireland, Jews and Arabs in the Middle East, Turks and Greeks on Cyprus, Hindus and Moslems in India, Americans and Russians, men and women everywhere— all have stereotyped views of one another that seem to make peaceful and mutually self-satisfying relations impossible.

Many of these cultural expectations and values are contrary to Christian values and hopes, but they are so ingrained in us that we are often not even aware that we have them. Moreover, if one of our stereotypes were to be challenged, we could easily defend it with examples. "Communists are godless atheists; you can't expect them to keep their word; moreover, look what they did in Hungary." "Catholics are only interested in conversion to their religion; if they take over a government, they will restrict the liberties of people of other religions. If you don't believe it, just look at the constitution of Italy or of the Republic of Ireland." Politicians play on our stereotypes and our concomitant fears of the "others" to win votes and pass bills. Both Russia and the United States are heading toward bankruptcy through enormous stockpiling of weapons and new weapons research; yet the leaders of both countries justify the madness as "defense" against an untrustworthy other. The social and cultural dimensions of our existence, in many ways, make it very difficult to live out the command of Jesus, "Love one another."

If depression, addiction or dysfunctional familial dynamics can appear so insoluble as to seem demonic, how much more so the enormous social, political, cultural and international problems faced by our modern world. First of

all, we are often not even aware that we are culturally bi-
ased and addicted. In the *Spiritual Exercises* Ignatius notes
that "when the enemy of our human nature tempts a just
soul with his wiles and seductions, he earnestly desires that
they be received secretly and kept secret." The "enemy"
need not worry ordinarily about our cultural and social
prejudices and addictions. As long as we keep to our accustomed paths, read our accustomed books and newspapers,
hobnob with our usual neighbors and co-workers, our biases will tend to operate without our awareness.

Secondly, even if we become aware of our own cultural biases, it can seem impossible to do anything about
them. "What good does it do for me to become convinced
of the basic humanity and decency of my Protestant neigh-
bor if both of our communities will ostracize us if we become friends?" "It's true that our family is wasteful and
overconsumes scarce resources, but our children will feel
deprived if we don't buy what every other child in the
neighborhood has."

Thirdly, the complexity and magnitude of the inter-
locking social, cultural, political and religious institutions
that need to be changed can render us immobile, make us
feel impotent. The feeling is caught by the phrase, "You
can't change City Hall." How can we individuals, even in
a democratic country, really change attitudes and values
so that it will be more possible for people of different races
and nationalities to love one another? A pipe dream indeed!

Sebastian Moore suggests that the voice of original sin
in us whispers things like: "Mistrust between men and
women is natural; it can't be changed"; "Poverty for some
people is just the way things are and have to be"; "Original
sin makes trust between nations impossible and wars inevi-
table." The voice of original sin, in other words, tries to get
us to believe not only that we cannot change City Hall but
that it may be sinful to try. Moore, however, notes:

The "realism" that normalizes mistrust is a false realism. . . . of course it is! For it is the "realism" of original sin. It is the realism you get when original sin, the flight from understanding, is allowed full sway. It is a "realism" that would bury civilization in radioactive rubble. I've heard it called "crackpot realism." It has a fatal appeal for a certain type of politician. Jacques Maritain was pointing to this pernicious pseudo-realism when he said that the worst thing we have inherited from Machiavelli is the notion—very prevalent today—that morality, trust, decent behaviour, is for idealists and does not belong in the market place and in politics. Anyone who believes this is listening to the voice of original sin, the original lie about the human condition. . . (*Let This Mind Be in You*).

With these examples, I hope we can see how strongly we can be influenced away from Christian values by the social, political, cultural and religious ambience in which we live and move and have our being. I say "religious" ambience as well, because so much of religious preaching and teaching is couched in exclusionary language. It is only recently, for example, that the Roman Catholic liturgy for Good Friday removed the offensive "perfidious Jews" from the great petitions. It is doubtful too that the Holocaust could have occurred without an atmosphere of anti-Semitism among Christians. Coming closer to home we can ask: What is the effect on the attitudes of both men and women toward women that the Roman Catholic Church tries to keep females of all ages from meaningful service at the eucharistic table? Moreover, in "missionary" countries, Christians are a scandal by their sectarian divisions and their attacks on one another. There are many attitudes inimical to the values of Jesus that are inculcated by the Christian churches.

How can we exorcise these social-cultural demons?

First, we need to know that we are "possessed" by them. We need to pray with as much vigor for the grace to know these demons as we pray to know the intra- and interpersonal demons that lead us astray. Perhaps the last words of Psalm 139 take on a new meaning when we are aware of the social-cultural dimension of our existence.

> Search me, O God, and know my heart;
> test me and know my anxious thoughts.
> See if there is any offensive way in me,
> and lead me in the way everlasting (Ps 139: 23-24).

This prayer might be enhanced by group prayer and reflection along the lines suggested by James Hug and Rose Marie Scherschel in a little booklet, *Social Revelation*, put out by the Center of Concern in Washington, D.C.

Secondly, we can change our usual patterns. For example, we can read a different newspaper, spend time with people of a different cultural, social, ethnic or religious group, get to know a foreign country firsthand and try to see our own country through the eyes of foreigners. Changes of pattern like these can bring to awareness our social-cultural biases.

Thirdly, once aware we must pray that the demons be driven out by the Lord's grace. We need to pray for a faith that can move mountains, a faith that we can make a difference by taking on the values of Jesus and trying with his grace to live them out. Here again, group reflection and prayer along the lines suggested by Hug and Scherschel and by the *"communidades de base"* of Latin America may help to overcome the tendencies to pay more heed to the voice of original sin than to the voice of Jesus and his Spirit.

Finally, in facing these demons of the social-cultural realm we need to take to heart as nowhere else the words of Jesus: "This kind can only come out by prayer" (Mk 9:29), and perhaps also these other words that counseled common prayer: ''Again, I tell you that if two of you on earth agree about anything you ask for, it will be done for you by my Father in heaven. For where two or three come together in my name, there am I with them'' (Mt 18:19-20).

12

The Church in the Modern World

Imagine this scene. Pope John XXV has just visited the Cathedral of Canterbury and concelebrated the Eucharist with the Archbishop of Canterbury. The event was a surprise to all, but word of its occurrence quickly spread as the media converged on the scene. Only two members of the Roman Curia, close confidants of the Pope, knew what he intended. The rest of the curial cardinals are aghast and some are quite angry. Pope John returns to Rome and meets with the cardinals in a closed-door session. They rather testily ask him to explain himself. He says: "A week ago I was praying, and I had a vision in which I was offerred communion by an Anglican bishop. I started to refuse, but heard a voice say, 'This is my body; take and eat.' It happened three times. Right after that I got a phone call from the Archbishop of Canterbury who told me that while he was praying he heard a voice tell him, 'Invite the Pope to concelebrate at Canterbury.' So I consulted with my two closest confidants, and I went. During the liturgy the Archbishop and I and those around us felt the powerful presence of the Holy Spirit."

I leave it to my readers to imagine the reactions among the cardinals. I have another purpose in mind. As mind-boggling as this scenario may seem, something like it seems to have happened in the early church (cf. Acts 10—11). I invite readers to reflect on that event and to apply the reflections to our own lives.

In the early chapters of the *Acts of the Apostles* the nascent church looked much like a Jewish sect. Its center was Jerusalem and the Temple. It would seem that the earliest converts were all Jews or converted Jews. The followers of Jesus were observers of the Torah, avoiding unclean foods and close contact with Gentiles. Circumcision for males was required. As we approach chapter 10, however, we begin to sense that pressure is building up. The persecution in Jerusalem has intensified. Paul has been converted. The good news is spreading rapidly beyond the confines of the Holy Land, and it is becoming harder to keep it within the bounds of Judaism. Yet adherence to the Law is unquestioned. One thinks of a pressure cooker holding in more and more powerful forces of expansion.

How did the early church break out of that pressure cooker without exploding into a thousand warring sects? That is the question, it seems to me, that the writer of Acts wants to answer in chapters 10 and 11. (I invite you to read those chapters at this point.)

The shift did not occur by a revolution, a power grab, or a political process of compromise, but by revelation. The writer of Acts describes an intervention of God while two men are praying. Cornelius, while pious and obviously positively inclined toward Judaism, is an uncircumcized Gentile. Yet at prayer he is told to send for Peter, and without hesitation he does. The next day as Cornelius' men near Joppa, Peter, too, is at prayer and in a trance has a vision in which he is told to kill unclean animals and eat. To imagine his horror we have to think of what it would be like to be asked to desecrate a crucifix or the Blessed Sacrament. While he ponders the meaning of this threefold vision, Cornelius' agents arrive, and a voice tells Peter to go with them. He receives these Gentiles into his house, and the next day accompanies them to the house of Cornelius. There the Holy Spirit comes on all those who hear Peter speak even before they are baptized. ''The circumcized believers who had come with Peter were astonished that the gift of the Holy Spirit had been poured out even on the Gentiles'' (Acts 10:45). So Peter believes that his own vision is confirmed, and he orders them to be baptized.

When Peter returns to Jerusalem, things are rather tense. ''. . .(T)he circumcized believers criticized him and said, 'You went into the house of uncircumcized men and ate with them' '' (Acts 11:2-3). One can feel the tension crackling in the air. Peter had made himself unclean; perhaps he should be shunned. Amazingly, all that Peter does is to tell them about his own and Cornelius' experiences in prayer and about what happened when he got to Cornelius' house. He does not engage in theological or philosophical argument; he just tells them what happened. ''When they heard this, they had no further objections and praised God, saying, 'So then, God has granted even the Gentiles repentance unto life' '' (Acts 11:18).

The book of Acts probably idealizes the reality of the early church. No doubt tensions between Gentile and Jewish Christians remained, and some churches probably ended up as sects. But the whole church did remain one at a very volatile moment in its history.

With my opening scenario I did not intend to lay the groundwork for a prophetic call to the Pope and the Archbishop of Canterbury. My purpose rather was to help us to imagine the scene in Acts. But now I do want to invite some reflections that bring home the point of this contemplation of Acts 10 and 11. My first point has to do with the state of the church at large; the second speaks to a way of discussing serious issues in the church.

The Roman Catholic Church of our century has been in a situation analogous to that of the early church. Up to the Second Vatican Council uniformity and adherence to law characterized it. No matter where one went in the world one experienced the same liturgy. Seminarians from one country could rather easily study in another because Latin was the common language and the textbooks were interchangeable. In Japan, in Brazil, in Sierra Leone, in Paris the only major differences one would encounter in a Roman Catholic Church would be the skin color of the worshipers and the language they spoke outside church. The vestments of the priests and altar boys, the hymns, the incense, the vigil lights and statues, even the message of the sermons would vary little from country to country. Roman Catholicism world-wide presented an image of monolithic culture and orthodoxy. The analogy of the Jewishness of the early church does not miss the mark by much.

At the same time, and almost unnoticed by most Catholics, the pot was boiling more and more furiously. The working classes of most of Europe had abandoned the church. The Modernist crisis of the early part of the century had been contained by strong, authoritarian measures, but the issues raised still percolated below the surface. The modern world with its new ways of looking at reality, of doing science, of asking questions would not go away. In spite of forceful measures by the Biblical Commission early in this century biblical scholarship was making itself felt even in Catholic seminaries, raising questions about the authorship of the Bible, its inerrancy, and its historical accuracy. Modern historical studies took some of the gilt off our images of popes and bishops. The horrors of two world wars with the use of poison gas, pattern bombing of cities, and the concentration camps cast doubt on the wisdom and the depth of European Christianity as the arbiter of theological, moral and spiritual values. The population explosion and the awareness of the disparities between the First and Third Worlds raised all sorts of questions about sexual and social ethics. Moreover, the emergence of a new world consciousness as well as of the plurality of cultures and of world religions made us wonder how we could live together on this planet endangered by the technology that produced among other things the atom and hydrogen bombs. And Christian missionary activity began to look more critically at itself in the light of this new world consciousness. No doubt there were many other factors at work; my point is that, like the early church in Acts, Roman Catholicism after World War II was experiencing tremendous ferment. The pressure cooker was at flash point.

Pope John XXIII's decision to call a council took the Catholic world by surprise. He and the bishops who assembled at the Vatican in 1962 must have been even more surprised by what happened there. The original schemata proposed by the various curial offices were found wanting, and a wholly new agenda developed. It would be naive to say that Pope John and Pope Paul VI and the assembled bishops of Vatican II heard a vision while in prayer. At Vatican II a good deal of political infighting no doubt occurred. Yet it is, I believe, not naive, but a matter of faith, to affirm that the Holy Spirit was at work and that these bishops, sinners like ourselves, did pray and did listen to the voice of the Spirit. The results were the decrees of Vatican II which radically changed the face of the Roman Catholic Church.

These decrees were not perfect. Nor was their implementation back home in the dioceses and parishes anywhere near perfect. Catholics were not well prepared pastorally to understand and internalize the changes. Schisms did occur, and some Catholics just drifted away. But the church as a whole did remain one and in the process became more catholic, more universal and pluriform. We were shaken, unquestionably, and we are still trying to assimilate all that has happened. Yet, we Roman Catholics are, as a whole, more involved with the modern world, more a force to be reckoned with in the shaping of that world as a result of the changes brought about by Vatican II. Like the early church we are now on course to meet the challenges of the world.

I invite readers to reflect on Acts 10 and 11 and our present situation. We need to let the Lord's Spirit convert us to the mindset obtained by the bishops of Vatican II. The good news of Jesus Christ needs to be heard by all people in our world. As we ponder that good news and let it penetrate to the marrow of our being, we, too, will realize, as the bishops of Vatican II must have, that "the light shines in the darkness, and the darkness has not overcome it" (Jn 1:5). As more and more of us experience the strength of that light and the goodness of that news, we will as a church have "no more objections" to the call of the Council and move out confidently into our world with the message that this world so desperately needs.

My second point invites reflection on the methodology of Acts 10-11. Even though I did not intend my opening scenario as a prophetic call to the present Pope and Archbishop of Canterbury, it would be refreshing to hear religious leaders speak of their experience in prayer when they announce decisions that affect the members of their churches and congregations. As noted earlier, Peter did not resort to quotations from the Old Testament or from Jesus or from earlier speeches of the apostles with arguments about their relevance to his situation with Cornelius. Rather he presented—to a rather hostile audience— experiences of prayer and of the aftermath of prayer. The audience listened and were satisfied that God had spoken.

An aside: Notice that Peter describes his actual experience. Such a description is quite different from the statement: "In my prayer I realized what God's will is." The latter is not a description of experience and can only be accepted unquestioningly or rejected. It cannot be tested by the group.

This scene may be one of the first recorded instances of group discernment of spirits, that is, of a group listening to experiences of prayer and discerning, as a group, that these experiences were experiences of God rather than delusions. It would take us too far afield at present to discuss the complexities and difficulties of group discernment. But it may be of help to groups that are dealing with sensitive is-

sues to indicate some ways of adapting the methodology
presented in Acts.

First, a group dealing with such an issue, where a vari-
ety of deeply held convictions exist, needs to be reminded
that Christians begin arguments and discussions with a
presupposition of the good will of the other members of the
group. Ignatius of Loyola had experienced much prejudice
when he first began to "give" his spiritual exercises. As a
result he put at the beginning of his book this note:

> To assure better cooperation between the one who
> is giving the *Exercises* and the exercitant, and more
> beneficial results for both, it is necessary to suppose
> that every good Christian is more ready to put a
> good interpretation on another's statement than to
> condemn it as false. If an orthodox construction can-
> not be put on a proposition, the one who made it
> should be asked how he understands it. If he is in
> error, he should be corrected with all kindness. If
> this does not suffice, all appropriate means should
> be used to bring him to a correct interpretation, and
> so defend the proposition from error.

In the case of the kind of group we are discussing, the presupposition might be expanded to presume that all the
other members of the group want sincerely to discover
God's will and are willing to pray to hear God speaking. If I
presuppose such an attitude in everyone else, then I will be
more open to hear their experience as possibly pointing to
God's will for us. Hence, I will listen differently even to
those in the group whose ideas are foreign to my own. Peter's audience, in spite of their hostility to what he had
done, must have had such an attitude.

It helps, too, if the members of the group first spend
some time in private prayer before entering into the discussion or debate or argument. Each one might ask the Spirit
for guidance on what to say and how to say it and for open-

ness to other points of view. Peter's audience must have been prayerful and open to be able to listen to such a foreign experience and test its authenticity.

Finally, after every one has been heard and before a vote or sense of the group is taken, the group might take some more time for private prayer asking the help of the Holy Spirit. During that prayer period each reviews what was said and then tries to come to a decision which will be communicated to the group.

These suggestions do not preclude hard study of issues and options. I am not advocating a mindless trust in "prayer." Nor will following these suggestions guarantee that the group has found the will of God or that it will avoid serious conflict. But I do believe that many discussions in the church would be immeasureably enhanced if we took a leaf from the way the early church seems to have resolved a very serious issue. At the least we would be taking seriously the possibility of learning something new from our brothers and sisters in the Lord, just as Peter's audience learned something new.

∽☞ **13** ☜∽

Is This Plan or Activity of God?

The following meditation seems to follow nicely from the reflections we have just made on how we might go about communal discernment in the church. In it I present for reflection some experiences I have had in my ministry. I begin by citing three historical instances where women have felt a desire to do a ministry in the church and were, at least at first, frustrated in accomplishing that desire.

• In the splendid story of her life written at the insistence of her confessors Teresa of Avila recounts the foundation of her first reformed convent. She had been commanded by God to move ahead toward its foundation and all signs pointed toward the accomplishment of God's will. At the last moment the provincial of the Cistercians, who had already given his permission, suddenly ordered her not to proceed any further. What was her reaction? She writes:

> God was so gracious to me that none of this worried me in the slightest; I gave up the project as easily and happily as though it had cost me nothing. This nobody could believe, not even the very persons, given to prayer as they were, with whom I had to do: they supposed I must be very much distressed and ashamed—even my confessor could not really believe that I was not. It seemed to me that I had done all I possibly could to fulfill the Lord's command and that therefore I had no further obligation.

So I remained in my own house, quite content and happy. I could not, however, give up my belief that the task would be duly accomplished, and, though I was unable to forecast the means and knew neither how nor when the work would be done, I was quite sure that it would be done in time.

Teresa notes that in obedience to the command of the provincial and of her confessor she herself did nothing at the time to bring about the foundation. But others were not so prevented; a "saintly Dominican" and Teresa's own companion in the venture wrote to Rome to seek a way out of the impasse. The indult from Rome duly arrived and the reformed convent was begun.

• A number of years ago I was at a parish in the hill country of Jamaica. Another priest asked me to accompany him on his communion calls to the sick. We were to be guided by a spry and wiry grandmother, Miz Bunny, who regularly took the priests on these rounds up almost pathless hills to the huts where the old and the maimed who could not get to church waited to receive communion. At some point I had been told by a priest who had been long in Jamaica that women like Miz Bunny did not want to distribute communion themselves. As we labored up the hills I was deeply moved by her energy and enthusiasm and by her easy kindness and friendship with the elderly and the leprous. She made us feel at home with her people. At one point I asked her whether she would like to bring communion herself. Her face lit up with a joyful smile and she quietly said: "Oh, yes, Father!" I was delighted to hear that her desire has finally been fulfilled. She now brings communion to the shut-ins herself.

• The final vignette is supplied by the life of Thérèse of Lisieux. In her autobiography she writes: "And at the same time I want to be a priest." The strength of this desire is revealed in her last conversations. Thérèse had told her sister

Céline even before she became sick that she would die in
1897, at the age of 24. Then in June, three months before her
death, she said to Céline: "Don't you see that God is going
to take me at an age when I would not have had the time to
become a priest. If I had been able to become a priest, it
would have been in this month of June, at this ordination
that I would have received holy orders. So in order that I
may regret nothing, God is allowing me to be sick; I
wouldn't have been able to present myself for ordination,
and I would have died before having exercised my ministry."

These three women felt strong desires to carry out a
task and were thwarted. Yet, all three remained relatively
peaceful, bouyant and faithful when their desires were
frustrated. These desires were not in the public domain.
Two of the three saw their desires fulfilled in spite of the
initial frustration. Thérèse of Lisieux interpreted her illness
and impending death as a sign of God's loving care to keep
her from regret.

Not all women who have experienced the desire for
priesthood have died early. In the contemporary Roman
Catholic Church in the United States and elsewhere there are
hundreds of women who identify with Thérèse's desire.
They feel that God has called them to ordained ministry in the
church, and they find themselves unable to follow through on
the Lord's call because of the stance of authority in the
church. Many have left the Roman Catholic Church for other
churches; others have just left institutional religion. I want to
talk about some women who remain convinced that their call
to priesthood is genuine, but who continue to minister joyfully and unreservedly in the church though, like Teresa of
Avila, they have their times of darkness and doubt.

For a number of years I have been a co-worker in ministry with and sometimes spiritual director to a number of
women who feel so called. Their experiences are not in the

public domain, nor do these women want to publicize themselves. Yet, I believe, the church needs to know about their experience as part of its ongoing discernment of what God is trying to accomplish. Theological and historical studies are important for the ongoing life of the church as are authoritative pronouncements. Equally important for its life is shared experience. If Teresa's hopes and dreams had not made their way to Rome, would God's desires for a reformed Carmelite order have been frustrated? If church leaders had not heard the desire of many lay people to become eucharistic ministers and had not seen the need, would God's desires for Miz Bunny have been thwarted? Who is to say? I do know that I have felt some urgency to try to get into the public domain the experience of the women with whom I have worked. The urgency is compounded by the growing realization that many of God's people are being deprived of Eucharist because of the dearth of priests. As more and perhaps different experiences become part our of our shared life the church will gain more clarity about God's intentions. The words of Gamaliel echo in my mind: ''Men of Israel, consider carefully what you intend to do to these men. . . . For if their purpose or activity is of human origin, it will fail. But if it is from God,. . . you will only find yourselves fighting against God'' (Acts 5:35-39).

It may be important to know a bit of my own background. Since 1969 I have been involved in training programs for ordained and non-ordained ministry, including an intensive and selective program for training spiritual directors. For six years I was vice-provincial for formation of the New England Jesuits. During these years I have met both men and women who desired priesthood who seemed to me unqualified. Some had no idea of what it might take to become sufficiently trained to be a priest. Some struck me as psychologically too immature to be considered for any professional ministry in the church. Some seemed too angry and power-hungry.

The women I have in mind are quite different. They are psychologically mature, having only the minor neuroses to which we are all subject. Moreover, they are exceptionally gifted ministers of the word when they teach or preach, and they are among the best spiritual directors I know. They have also gone to great lengths, and not without suffering, to obtain the theological and ministerial training necessary for their ministry. Some have had leadership roles in religious congregations and their ages range from the forties to the seventies.

Each of the women I have in mind has been praying seriously for years and has sought regular and competent spiritual direction. Each makes at least an eight-day directed retreat every year, and a number have also made the full Spiritual Exercises (30 days) under capable direction. Those whose prayer experience I know best have developed a relationship of intimacy with God and his Son Jesus that has moved from the discernment of the beginner to that of a companion of the Lord. They have asked to be with Jesus on mission, even on dangerous mission, and have been consoled by his acceptance of their desire. They open themselves honestly and humbly to their spiritual directors and look for challenge because they want to follow their Lord and not go up a garden path. In other words, they are continually testing the spirits as best they can. They ask the Lord whether they are deluding themselves about the desire for priesthood since the door seems to be even more firmly closed now than ten years ago. Nothing in their prayer experience points toward such a discernment of delusion. In fact, the opposite seems to be the case. To want to give up the sense of call seems to bring on desolation and a sense of moving away from close companionship with the Lord.

Moreover, nothing in their day-to-day life of ministry points to delusion either. They are rather remarkably buoyant and, as far as I can tell, well-liked and cherished by those with whom they live and work. They experience consolation and hope in spite of continually running into situations that face them with the frustration of their desires. A number of these women have had experiences where someone to whom they were ministering said after a particularly revealing session: "I wish you were a priest so I could receive absolution right now." They have urged such people to seek out a priest for absolution, sometimes over the person's objections. All of them regularly do team ministry with priests and thus regularly feel the exclusion from the altar when the priest celebrates the liturgy. All have led groups of women religious or lay people in faith-sharing, community building, or communal discernment when a priest, almost inevitably a stranger to the process, has to be asked to celebrate and preach at the closing liturgy. Frequently enough these women attend liturgies and hear homilies that are poorly prepared and know that the people could be better served. They complain to the Lord of such experiences of frustration, but they do not lose heart or a sense of humor. Nor do they turn away in anger and resentment from the church that seems to frustrate their deepest call. They really do seem to feel as Teresa did for the most part when God's plans for a reformed convent seemed to be scuttled. They are not threatening to leave the church. They, like Teresa, seem to be able to go on with their lives of prayer and service without much resentment at all.

All my instincts, training and experience lead me to the conclusion that these women are experiencing an authentic call of God. Their experience leads them to more and more self-abnegation and selfless service of the people of God. They are not hung up on priesthood, but they do feel that the Lord wants to use them as priests. The road so far has not been a dead end because they have become more and more effective and gifted servants of the Lord and his people. It could be that the concrete detail of "priesthood" will be found to be illusory in the sense that it will not come in their lifetimes. Legitimate authority in the church will decide that. One woman wrote to me: "I have a strong desire to be a priest, but know that my age would be a factor for me. I believe that it will come—priesthood for women—but probably not in my time. However, I console myself by being priest in my heart in all that I do now."

All of us in the church need to take seriously the experiences of women such as I have described. Is God saying something to us about ministry in the church through them? And if so, what is he saying? In *Experience and God* John E. Smith affirms the necessity of shared experience for a religious community: "A living religion, or rather a religion which hopes to save its life, cannot ultimately afford to avoid the critical test of shared experience. On the contrary, from shared experience comes its life." So too new life for the church's ministry may only come by reflecting on shared experience.

⟨⟨⟨ Part Four ⟩⟩⟩

Death and Resurrection

Often in this book we have touched upon the role of fear in blocking us from developing our relationship with God and from living out the dream of God. A few times I alluded to the idea that at the root of our fears is the fear of death. The following two chapters take up the theme of dying and rising directly and provide a fitting conclusion to the book.

⚶ 14 ⚶

A Meditation on Death and Life

"... whenever it is a damp, drizzly November in my soul..." These opening words of *Moby Dick* strike a responsive chord in those of us who live in northern climes. We know how bleak November days can be. For us it seems natural to celebrate the feasts of All Saints and All Souls in November and to end the liturgical calendar near the end of this month or at the beginning of December. I have often wondered how the liturgical calendar fares in the southern hemisphere when November is the heart of spring. Be that as it may, the November weather and its feast days do face us with the end of life and with the end of the world (whatever that might mean). I propose that in these last two chapters we meditate on the "last things."

In his Pulitzer Prize-winning book, *The Denial of Death*, Ernest Becker says: "... the idea of death, the fear of it, haunts the human animal like nothing else; it is a mainspring of human activity—activity designed largely to avoid the fatality of death, to overcome it by denying in some way that it is the final destiny for man (sic)." He then goes on to argue that this denial is so pervasive and pernicious that it is *the* source of our modern psychic and social ills, and he makes a very good case for his argument.

Death faces us with annihilation, the loss of self and all that gives meaning to life. What I fear depends, of course, on what I see as myself. If I am my body, then I will do everything to preserve it. Is this fear behind the cult of the body in our culture? If I am my family or race, then I will do

115

everything to preserve them. In our century we have seen the horrors to which a cult of family or race or country can lead. Rather than explore these different ways of defining the self, I would like to assume, with John Macmurray, that to be a person is to be in relationship, that the unit of the personal is the I and the You. With this assumption I will explore the fear of death and what Christian faith invites us to experience.

Without some "you" I am not a person, says Macmurray. In other words, I need you (and you and you . . .) in order to be myself. To get an inkling of the truth of this statement, recall how we cling to important relationships even when they are destructive or when the clinging is destructive. If the statement is true, then what I most fear in dying is the loss of all relationships, which would be the equivalent to the annihilation of myself. Thus the fear of death is fear for oneself and vice-versa.

Yet to be human is to die. But, someone may argue, death entered the world of the human only with sin. Some modern theologians would, however, say that sin did not bring death into the world; rather, sin changed the way death is experienced. This is, for example, the argument of Sebastian Moore in *Let This Mind Be in You*. In other words, because of sin death, which is human destiny, part of what it means to be human, is experienced as the threat of annihilation. In this understanding, God, the creator of the universe, in his goodness created human beings whose reality included dying. Hence, death is not annihilation, but the final consummation of life and an opening to more life. Death, then, is not the loss of all relationships, but an opening to much wider and deeper relationships. Sin makes the experience dreadful, not creation itself.

To get a purchase on this notion, let us look at the death of Jesus. Jesus, as the sinless one, has no illusions, no rationalizations. He has no progeny as he faces death. He can intuit the doom that faces his people from the Romans, so he cannot comfort himself with the triumph of his race. He is betrayed by one of his closest friends, denied by another, and abandoned by all. His body is stripped of all dignity; crucifixion is a horrible way to die. His mission is a failure; he is mocked and derided by Jew and Roman alike. Even God seems distant as he cries out: "My God, my God, why have you forsaken me?" The universe seems to hold its breath. Will he accept what Tolkien calls the "doom of men" willingly, with trust and love? Or will he finally despair? Luke's gospel seems to capture this feeling. "It was now about the sixth hour, and darkness came over the whole land until the ninth hour, for the sun stopped shining. And the curtain of the temple was torn in two" (Lk 23: 44-45). We sense the sigh of relief of the universe as Jesus calls out with a loud voice: "Father, into your hands I commit my spirit" and breathes his last (v. 46).

Sebastian Moore speaks of the chosen passion, not in the sense that Jesus as the sinless one did not have to die, but rather in the sense that Jesus trustingly accepted the "doom of men." He trusted that God *is* his (and our) Abba (dear Father, dear Mother) and that not even death could change who God is. If God is, for all eternity, our Abba, then Jesus and we will be for all eternity God's sons and daughters.

Thus Jesus was the most fully human person who ever lived because he accepted with trust and love the full reality of being human which included accepting the truth that death is the only way to be fully human. In Macmurray's terms Jesus trusted that he would always be a person even through death, that he would always be in relationship. In fact, only through death could he be more a person, in more relationships, deeper and stronger relationships, not only with Abba, but with all of his brothers and sisters who had gone before him and would come after him.

Perhaps we can now understand better the profound meaning of these words in John's gospel:

"The hour has come for the Son of Man to be glorified. I tell you the truth, unless a kernel of wheat
falls to the ground and dies, it remains only a single
seed. But if it dies, it produces many seeds. The man
who loves his life will lose it, while the man who
hates his life in this world will keep it for eternal life.
Whoever serves me must follow me; and where I
am, my servant also will be. My Father will honor
the one who serves me.

"Now my heart is troubled, and what shall I say?
'Father, save me from this hour'? No, it was for this
very reason I came to this hour. Father, glorify your
name!" (Jn 12:23-28).

The only way that Jesus can live, that is, be more fully a person, be glorified, is to die. So in a real sense he does "go
gentle into that good night;" he does choose death.

For the disciples, of course, the crucifixion was the
shipwreck of all their hopes. We can hear the pathos in the
words of the two disciples who met the stranger on the road
to Emmaus: "But we had hoped that he was the one who
was going to redeem Israel" (Lk 24:21). They had lost the
one You who gave meaning to all their I's. With him gone
who were they? Yet in this very moment of despair something happens that makes their hearts burn within them.
They meet a stranger on the road. Could it be? Whatever it
was, they did not want to let this stranger out of their company, and they prevailed on him to stay and eat with them.
They felt all the old stirrings of life and warmth and challenge and hope that—Could it be?—they had felt in Jesus'
presence. "When he was at the table with them, he took
bread, gave thanks, broke it and began to give it to them.
Then their eyes were opened and they recognized him, and
he disappeared from their sight" (Lk 24:30-31).

With this experience they had themselves back, as it
were. The one You who made all the difference to who they
are is alive and well. And the vital importance of these first

witnesses for us is that they testify that they are experiencing the same Jesus whom they walked and talked and ate with, the same Jesus whom they had abandoned or denied, the same Jesus whom they had seen die so horribly. Thus, they assure us that the Jesus whom we experience in prayer, in reading the gospels, in the sacrament of reconciliation, in the Eucharist is Jesus of Nazareth, Mary's son.

For that is the heart of the matter in any November time, damp and drizzly or not. Our hearts do burn within us at times. We do sense the presence of the mysterious Other whom we name Jesus, and we know with faith and hope and love, at least in those moments, that death has no sting. In those moments we have no doubts either that it is right for the church to celebrate the feast of All Saints because we know that no one who has died in Christ is lost, annihilated. Rather we know that ''we are surrounded by such a great cloud of witnesses'' (Heb 12:1) that we have even more relationships than we could ever count. In those moments, too, we know that it is right for the church to celebrate the feast of All Souls, because we can hope that all our loved ones are, like Mary, in Christ and, therefore, whole and entire and in relationship with us and everyone else. Indeed, it may be a measure of our faith and hope that we pray to (that is, converse with) not only Jesus, Mary and the saints, but also to those of our loved ones who have gone before us into that good night.

Because we can have experiences of God the Father, of Jesus, of the Spirit, of Mary, of the saints and of our loved ones who are saints we can say with St. Paul:

What, then, shall we say in response to this? If God is for us, who can be against us? He who did not spare his own Son, but gave him up for us all—how will he not also, along with him, graciously give us all things? . . . . For I am convinced that neither death nor life, neither angels nor demons, neither

the present nor the future, nor any powers, neither
height nor depth, nor anything else in all creation,
will be able to separate us from the love of God that
is in Christ Jesus our Lord (Rom 8:31-39).

Perhaps at such times we can even say that death is not the
doom of humankind, but our boon. For only death will take
away the blinders that keep us from seeing the whole of our
reality, that we are in communion with all human beings
because we are in communion with the eternal community,
Father, Son, and Spirit, the one mystery we call God.

ᒡᕮ **15** ᕮᕐᓄ

Experiences of Dying and Rising

In the preface to his *True Resurrection,* H. A. Williams argues that "theological inquiry is basically related to self-awareness and that therefore it involves a process of self-discovery so that, whatever else theology is, it must in some sense be a theology of the self." On this assumption we do not know what theological terms mean unless we can make personal sense of them. Indeed, Williams maintains that the term "resurrection" means very little to modern Christians or post-Christians precisely because Christians have removed from its understanding any reference to our personal present. He says in the body of his text: "When therefore resurrection is considered in terms of past and future, it is robbed of its impact on the present." To have present impact, the resurrection of Jesus must not be understood only as an event that happened to Jesus 2,000 years ago and that we hope will happen to each of us after our death. Resurrection must be understood and be experienced as personal, as affecting our lives now. Moreover, to be credible in our age, whatever may be true of other ages, the resurrection must be experienced not only within the individual but also between individuals and groups of individuals.

A theology and a catechesis which presented the resurrection as having only past or future relevance have, no doubt, contributed to the present state of general indifference toward resurrection. But there may be more at work here than catechetical or theological mistakes. Accepting personal or interpersonal or social resurrection may not be as easy as we sometimes believe. We may not be able to experience the joy of resurrection because we have to accept the reality of what precedes it, namely, a death of some kind. On the road to Emmaus Jesus says to the two disciples who are so downcast: "How foolish you are, and how slow of heart to believe all that the prophets have spoken! Did not the Christ have to suffer these things and then enter his glory?" (Lk 24: 25-26). If we cannot accept in all its cruelty Jesus' passion and death, still evident in the wounds in his hands, feet and side, we cannot really enjoy his present glory. In this chapter I want to illustrate both the presence of resurrection and the necessity of accepting the reality of suffering and death in order to experience it.

Since I began by arguing with H. A. Williams that we need to look to our experience to grasp the real meaning of the resurrection, I want to use my own experiences of death and resurrection. As I pondered my experience, three events stood out as exemplary of others in the same category. Each involved a real sense of dying; indeed, the "rising" could not have occurred if the dying had not been recognized and acknowledged. Yet one seemed to involve only myself, the second myself and someone else, and the third a community of people. Hence, I could point to experiences of resurrection that were personal, interpersonal and communal. Without further ado let me describe each.

• Once I was emotionally devastated by a turn taken in a relationship with a very close friend. With my intellect I could accept the change that was taking place, but my emotions mightily rebelled. I was filled with feelings of self-pity and resentment which I knew were self-defeating and immature, but I could not shake them. Nor was there anything my friend could do to help me since the change had to take place. I turned to the Lord for healing.

My spiritual director suggested that I use some of the

healing passages in the gospels as material for prayer. I read the passage where two blind men follow Jesus asking him to have mercy (Mt 9: 27-31). When they come into the house with him, he turns to them and asks: "Do you believe that I am able to do this?" Immediately I knew that if I said "Yes" to this question, I would be healed; almost as immediately I recoiled from the desire to be healed. It seemed to me that if I accepted healing of my resentment and self-pity, I would also have to accept the change in the relationship. That hurt too much because in my blindness I felt that the change in the relationship meant losing my friend entirely. I could not accept the possible death of that friendship. The only prayer I could make was: "Help me to want to be healed." That prayer was the beginning of the move toward healing and wholeness. Gradually I came to accept the dying of the old relationship, and only then could a new and more mature friendship arise.

• A few years ago when I was vice-provincial in charge of the formation of younger Jesuits, I made my official yearly visit to one of the scholastics. In the course of our first conversation during the visit he told me that he could no longer trust me because of a decision I had made in his regard. By the grace of God I did not become overly defensive, angry or upset. After he had said all that he felt—and it took some time—we realized that we had a problem. I was the major superior of record, as it were, and we were stuck with one another until I finished my term. In the Jesuit ideal the relationship of superior and subject is supposed to be one of mutual trust. Needless to say, that seemed more than ordinarily difficult, if not impossible, in the present circumstances. So we agreed to spend some time in prayer and reflection and meet again the next day. The next day the atmosphere had noticeably changed. We were not out of the woods, but we both recognized that it took a significant amount of trust for him to tell me the truth about what he felt. I had to admire his courage; and he realized that his fears about my reactions had been unfounded. Something in each of us had to die before the new and deeper level of trust emerged from that tomb. In the years since we have been able to recall that encounter with a sense that something holy happened; we can also laugh at it; and he gave me permission to tell the story here. Note that if the reality of a dead or moribund relationship had not been acknowledged, no resurrection would have occurred.

• Once another Jesuit and I were asked to be facilitators for a community of religious men who wanted to engage in communal discernment. Perhaps it might be more accurate to say that their superior wanted the community to move toward communal discernment. Our first session with the community opened up a Pandora's box of anger, suspicion, pain, hurt and dismay. Community members blamed everyone but themselves for their troubles, from others in the community to past and present superiors. Some were dismayed that so much feeling had been unearthed and blamed the facilitators for opening the box. Not surprisingly, the meeting was not one of the high moments in the lives of either the community or the facilitators. We were as much at a loss as were the community members and wondered what could be done.

Stammering about, I said something like this: "Well, apparently this is the reality which we present to the Lord. If I were directing an individual who was feeling some of what you're feeling, I would ask the person to let the Lord know how he or she felt and to ask the Lord for healing or for whatever else he or she wanted." I then recalled the scene in the upper room in John's gospel (chapter 20) just before the risen Jesus appears. I suggested that they reflect on that scene; the apostles must have been lost, bewildered; they might have blamed one another for what had happened to Jesus; they may have felt guilty, afraid, dismayed. The community members might be able to identify with the apostles and to express to Jesus their feelings and to ask for his help. We suggested that they use this passage for prayer the next morning and return to the community room to report on what happened.

The next morning about three quarters of the community showed up even though it was a Saturday and the meeting was not originally scheduled. Many had to rearrange schedules in order to attend. This meeting had a totally different tone. The men spoke of their need for forgiveness and healing as a community and as individuals, of their hope that Jesus would be in their midst, of their real admiration for one another, of seeing things from a new perspective. They had not reached the promised land yet, but they were on their way toward becoming something more like a community which could deal openly with volatile decisions. As painful as the first session was, it was necessary that the reality of their brokenness as a community surface so that they could ask for healing and to experience the hope of the risen Jesus. If these feelings had not surfaced, they would not have known of their need.

We who believe in Jesus do experience in our lives the power of his resurrection. The burden of Williams' argument in *True Resurrection* is that Christians do experience the resurrection of body, mind and spirit in their actual lives. My own reflections bear him out. Moreover, I believe, we experience the resurrection not only within ourselves (intrapersonally), but also interpersonally and communally. And I would venture to say that the experience of communal resurrection is far more frequent than we are led to believe by our news media. Protestants and Catholics in Northern Ireland do pray together as well as tear one another apart. Jews and Arabs do become friends. In the often dog-eat-dog world of the inner cities of the world's metropolises people share what little they have and go out of their way to help one another.

What is needed to experience resurrection, however, is the unblinking recognition that we are dead or dying, that we are terribly in need of the unearned power of the resurrection. There's the rub. Too often we prefer the illusion of health or of peace at any price to the hard reality of our brokenness, our sinfulness, our death with its concomitant admission of our need for "amazing grace." Once again I am reminded of John Macmurray's trenchant comment on the difference between illusory and real religion.

> All religion . . . is concerned to overcome fear. We can distinguish real religion from unreal by contrasting their formulae for dealing with negative motivation. The maxim of illusory religion runs: "Fear not; trust in God and He will see that none of the things you fear will happen to you"; that of real religion, on the contrary, is "Fear not; the things that you are afraid of are quite likely to happen to you, but they are nothing to be afraid of."

"How foolish you are, and how slow of heart to believe all that the prophets have spoken! Did not the Christ have to suffer these things and then enter his glory?"

Annotated Bibliography

Ashwin, Angela, *Heaven in Ordinary: Contemplative Prayer in Ordinary Life*. Great Wakering, Essex, England: Mayhew McCrimmon, 1985. A wonderful little book that should be helpful to ordinary people like ourselves in our desire to pray.

Barry, William A., *God and You: Prayer as a Personal Relationship*. Mahwah, NJ: Paulist Press, 1987.

Barry, William A., *"Seek My Face": Prayer as a Personal Relationship in Scripture*. Mahwah, NJ: Paulist Press, 1989.

Becker, Ernest, *The Denial of Death*. New York: Free Press, 1973. An insightful and powerful Pulitzer Prize-winning book which pulls the scales from our eyes on how we try to avoid the reality of death.

Buechner, Frederick, *The Sacred Journey*. San Francisco: Harper & Row, 1982. An autobiographical memoir whose aim is to show how God has spoken in the ordinary events of his life. While referring to Buechner, I want to mention his novels which have also had a profound effect on my attitudes to the relationship to God, *The Book of Bebb*, *Godric* and *Brendan*. As does the fiction of Flannery O'Connor, Buechner's depicts people who take the relationship with God seriously. Humor and pathos clasp hands.

Hall, Thelma, *Too Deep for Words: Rediscovering Lectio Divina*. New York/Mahwah: Paulist Press, 1988. A very practical little book to help people pray with scripture. Includes 500 scripture texts for prayer.

Hanh, Thich Nhat, *Being Peace*. Berkeley, CA: Parallax, 1987. Some moving and profound meditations by a well-known Vietnamese Buddhist monk.

Hug, James E. and Scherschel, Rose Marie, *Social Revelation*. Washington, D.C.: Center for Concern, 1987. Practical ways to help groups to reflect prayerfully on the social issues of our day.

Macmurray, John, *The Self as Agent* and *Persons in Relation*. London: Faber and Faber, 1957 and 1961. The Gifford Lectures of 1953-54. A profound analysis of the problem of the personal in philosophy. Difficult and dense reading, but well worth the trouble.

Moore, Sebastian, *Let This Mind Be in You: The Quest for Identity Through Oedipus to Christ*. San Francisco: Harper & Row (Seabury), 1985. A dense, but brilliant work by one of the most original spiritual theologians writing today.

O'Connor, Flannery, *The Complete Stories*. New York: Farrar, Straus and Giroux, 1987. Her stories do wonders for one's spiritual life.

Shannon, William H., *Seeking the Face of God*. New York: Crossroad, 1988. A theologicaly sophisticated presentation of the prayer of *lectio divina* that is also practical and brings in the turn to social justice required of any modern spirituality worth its salt.

Thompson, William G., *The Gospels for Your Whole Life: Mark and John in Prayer and Study*. Minneapolis: Winston, 1983. A wonderfully practical book with suggestions for how to use the two gospels for prayer by a scripture scholar who writes well and personally.

Thompson, William G., *Paul and His Message for Life's Journey*. New York/Mahwah: Paulist Press, 1986. He does the same thing for Paul that he did for Mark and John.